THE GEORGE RODRIGUE FOUNDATION OF THE ARTS

WOULD LIKE TO EXPRESS THEIR APPRECIATION

TO THE FOLLOWING SPONSORS:

LouisianaTravel.com

RODRIGUE STUDIOS

LOUISIANA EDUCATION LOAN AUTHORITY

A D I V I S I O N O F L P F A

KEITH WILDHABER CHARITABLE FUND

THEIR SUPPORT HAS MADE THIS PUBLICATION POSSIBLE.

THE POT &
THE PALETTE
COOKBOOK II

DELICIOUS REGIONAL RECIPES WITH ARTWORK
BY LOUISIANA'S MOST TALENTED STUDENT ARTISTS

FOR THE BENEFIT OF THE GEORGE RODRIGUE FOUNDATION OF THE ARTS

GEORGE RODRIGUE

FOUNDATION OF THE ARTS

All proceeds from this book will directly benefit the programs of the George Rodrigue Foundation of the Arts.

Published in 2022 by George Rodrigue Foundation of the Arts
Copyright © 2022 George Rodrigue Foundation of the Arts

Cataloging-in-Publication Data has been applied for and may be obtained from the Library of Congress.

ISBN: 979-8-218-02190-0

Volume Editor: Diane Abrams
Editorial Coordinator: Christine Tassin Dunaway
Producers: Wayne Fernandez, Gus Anderson
Designer: Chris Thompson
Contributor: Louisiana Restaurant Association
Dedication: Chef Paul Prudhomme
Index: Jay Kreider
Consulting Editor: Jennifer Williams

Cover Design: Chris Thompson Designs NYC

The text of this book was composed in Minion and Veneer.

Printed and bound in Mexico, by Litográfica Ingramex.

10 9 8 7 6 5 4 3 2 1

KARMEN GALLARDO, *FEEDING CURIOSITY*, MIXED MEDIA. (Artwork on frontispiece)

CONTENTS

IN MEMORY OF
CHEF PAUL PRUDHOMME

Paul Prudhomme (1940-2015) was a world-renowned chef, restaurateur, author, and television personality who turned Louisiana Cajun and Creole cooking into a worldwide phenomenon. With signature dishes, such as his famous Blackened Redfish, he put Cajun food on the map, and through his relatable and entertaining television shows and cookbooks, he made it modern and accessible to home chefs. The dishes he created, just like his larger-than-life personality, were vibrant and bold. His restaurant, K-Paul's Louisiana Kitchen, was an international culinary destination for decades.

Chef Paul is also known for his immense generosity. He never shied away from lending a helping hand to friends or fellow chefs. During the aftermath of Hurricane Katrina in 2005, K-Paul's was one of the first restaurants in the city to reopen, and Chef Paul also fed thousands of people out of his warehouse during the recovery efforts. Ask those who knew him, and you will likely hear one great story after another, not only about his great food, but of his kind heart and generosity of spirit.

Today, Chef Paul's legacy continues through a company he founded and owned for more than 35 years—Magic Seasoning Blends. These exceptional seasoning blends, made with dried vegetables, herbs,

"GOOD COOKING.
GOOD EATING.
GOOD LOVING."™

—CHEF PAUL PRUDHOMME

and spices, can be found in 37 countries around the world. Within this cookbook, you will find three unique Chef Paul recipes, each showcasing a different blend of spices (Beef Vegetable Soup, page 53; Gingered Green Vegetables, page 127; and Sweet Potato Pecan Pie Squares with Chantilly Cream, page 154). You will also find Magic Seasoning Blends mentioned as the preferred spice blend to use in many other recipes throughout the cookbook.

If Chef Paul Prudhomme had an artist counterpart, it would be George Rodrigue. They grew up just a few towns over from one another in Cajun country, and both pursued a passion for their crafts from a young age, drawing from their culture as inspiration. Their contributions to art and cuisine have made a lasting mark in Louisiana, and beyond. It is remarkable that Chef Paul produced the first national book on Cajun cooking (*Chef Paul Prudhomme's Louisiana Kitchen*, 1984), while George Rodrigue produced the first national book on Cajun culture (*The Cajuns of George Rodrigue*, 1976). George and Chef Paul were friends for nearly thirty years and supported each other's talents and efforts at festivals, fundraisers, gallery exhibitions, and restaurant openings, sometimes even working side by side at events—George painted, while Chef Paul cooked.

In fact, George Rodrigue painted Chef Paul's portrait three times. The most famous

(opposite left, 1989) commemorates K-Paul's Louisiana Kitchen in New York City (now closed). George also painted Chef Paul in a large genre piece titled *The Great Cajun Omelet* (above, 1984), commemorating a long-held French tradition, which began in the South of France and continues in Abbeville, Louisiana to this day.

We are proud to dedicate this cookbook to the legacy and memory of Chef Paul Prudhomme.

A MESSAGE FROM LIEUTENANT GOVERNOR OF LOUISIANA, BILLY NUNGESSER

As Lieutenant Governor of Louisiana, it is my pleasure to share a personal glimpse of Louisiana through the many recipes highlighted in *The Pot & the Palette Cookbook II*. This cookbook includes over 100 recipes and stories from some of the top Louisiana chefs, restaurants and individuals from across the state. *The Pot & the Palette Cookbook II* features artwork by winners and participants of an annual art scholarship contest hosted by the George Rodrigue Foundation of the Arts. The first *The Pot & the Palette Cookbook* was so successful, the George Rodrigue Foundation published a second volume.

This is a perfect blending of art and culinary heritage that helps to define the many cultures of Louisiana. Each ingredient speaks its own language. Good food always brings big smiles and fond memories. A state like no other, Louisiana is a place for togetherness, celebration and happiness. We call it *"joie de vivre"* – joy of life.

I hope you enjoy the recipes in *The Pot & the Palette Cookbook II*, and I hope they become a family tradition in your home.

Bon appetit!

Billy Nungesser

Billy Nungesser

Feed Your Soul.

LouisianaTravel.com

ABOUT THE LOUISIANA RESTAURANT ASSOCIATION EDUCATION FOUNDATION

The Louisiana Restaurant Association Education Foundation (LRAEF) was founded in 1995 by the Louisiana Restaurant Association as a 501(c)3 non-profit organization to enhance the industry's service to the public through education, workforce development, and promotion of career opportunities. Since the foodservice industry is the largest employer in the state of Louisiana, the LRAEF is vital to cultivating the next generation of the culinary and management workforce. The LRAEF fulfills its mission through three programs: ProStart®, LRAEF Scholars, and Restaurant Youth Registered Apprenticeship (RYRA).

Louisiana ProStart is a culinary program for high school students that develops the best and brightest talent into tomorrow's industry leaders. From culinary techniques to management skills, ProStart's industry-driven curriculum provides real-world educational opportunities. Today, Louisiana ProStart includes more than 1,700 students at more than 50 schools throughout the state and is a Department of Education JumpStart program.

The LRAEF Scholars program further educates ProStart students, culinary/hospitality students, industry employees, and educators by providing financial support for post-secondary degrees and certificates. These Scholars have chosen the culinary and/or hospitality fields as a career choice or wish to continue to work in the industry. Post-secondary institutions that have benefited from this program include: Nicholls State University, University of New Orleans, Louisiana Culinary Institute, Delgado Community College, University of Holy Cross, Northwestern State University, and University of Louisiana at Lafayette. Since its inception, the LRAEF has distributed over $650,000.

The Restaurant Youth Registered Apprenticeship (RYRA) was established in 2020 in partnership with the National Restaurant Association Educational Foundation and the U.S. Department of Labor. RYRA is an "earn while you learn" training model that helps new hires and existing workers achieve skill mastery, earn an industry-recognized credential, and advance towards a career. The age demographic for potential employees is 17-24.

Through its three signature programs, the LRAEF is helping to grow the foodservice industry within the state of Louisiana and provide young people with viable career options that they may not have been exposed to otherwise. The LRAEF is preparing the next generation to enter exciting careers, where the options for growth are unparalleled.

THE GEORGE RODRIGUE FOUNDATION OF THE ARTS

The George Rodrigue Foundation of the Arts (GRFA), founded in 2009 as a non-profit 501(c)(3) organization, advocates the importance of the arts in all school curriculums and supports a variety of art education programs. Through George's Art Closet, one of the foundations signature programs, GRFA donates customized art kits to Louisiana art teachers and schools, whose funding does not otherwise allow for the expense, giving teachers the opportunity to provide meaningful arts experiences for their students. Over 200 schools have shared in more than $220,000 in art supply awards.

Through its Print Donation Program, GRFA makes available to other non-profits Estate Stamped prints by George Rodrigue. Not only does this program raise funds for GRFA programs, throughout the years, it also has helped to raise more than $3 million for other non-profits throughout Louisiana and nationally.

GRFA's Annual Scholarship Art Contest, now in its thirteenth year, has attracted 6,100 entries from nearly 150 Louisiana cities, and has awarded $555,000 in college scholarships and awards to more than 200 winners. In 2020, GRFA expanded the contest to include a scholarship songwriting contest in partnership with the Trombone Shorty Foundation. Each year's competition theme is determined by GRFA and is announced at the beginning of the school year. To encourage participation by all, there is no grade point average requirement and scholarship winners are not required to major in art. Artwork created by the winners has travelled for public exhibition to various locations, including the Shaw Center for the Arts in Baton Rouge, the R.W. Norton Gallery in Shreveport, and the Hilliard University Art Museum in Lafayette. In 2013 and again in 2022, artwork of the winners from the previous years' competition, appeared in GRFA's cookbooks, *The Pot & the Palette Cookbook*, volumes I and 2. Lyrics of the winning songs of 2022 appear in volume two.

In 2012, GRFA launched Louisiana A+ Schools (LAA+), a research-based whole school arts-integrated network. The A+ model encourages creativity and stimulates learning by incorporating the arts into every school subject by providing training and professional development for entire faculties. Currently operating in 25 schools statewide, Louisiana A+ Schools is a public 501(c)(3) organization supported by GRFA.

Continuing the legacy of artist George Rodrigue, under the direction of his son, GRFA's Executive Director, Jacques Rodrigue, the foundation continues to focus primarily on Louisiana schools through arts education initiatives and hopes to expand its reach through partnerships with schools and foundations nationwide.

THE 2022 ART AND SONGWRITING CONTEST

"Louisiana's Culinary Heritage," theme of the 2022 Annual Scholarship Art and Songwriting Contest, repeated the widely popular theme of the Foundation's 2013 Art Contest and was expanded to include a third annual Songwriting Contest (in partnership with the Trombone Shorty Foundation). Louisiana high school juniors and seniors were invited to submit their original work of art or a song highlighting the exceptional food culture of our state through its festivals, dishes, and local ingredients.

The contest drew more than 300 entries, and thirteen students were selected to share $25,000 in college scholarships. The finalists were chosen by a panel of judges that included artists, educators, curators, museum professionals, musicians, songwriters, and recording artists. In addition to winning scholarships, contest winners also were awarded with the opportunity to display their work in this cookbook.

The Pot & the Palette Cookbook II features more than 100 new recipes from chefs throughout Louisiana, the artwork and song lyrics of the 2022 finalists, as well as additional top-scoring artworks. Back in 2013, the Foundation published volume one, *The Pot & the Palette Cookbook,* featuring art from that year's annual scholarship art contest. We are proud to continue the legacy of George Rodrigue through these contests and cookbooks, which honor Louisiana chefs, artists, and songwriters.

Thank you to all the students who entered this year's contest, and thank you to the teachers and parents who supported these students along the way. And a big thank you to our sponsors (page 1) who helped to make this cookbook possible!

CHAPTER ONE
APPETIZERS

New Iberia ★

MAKES 5 CUPS

¼ cup fresh rosemary leaves

¼ cup olive oil

2 tablespoons sugar

2 teaspoons kosher salt

1 tablespoon fresh cracked black pepper

5 cups Cane River Mammoth Pecan Halves

ROSEMARY ROASTED PECANS
CANE RIVER PECAN COMPANY

These fresh rosemary flavored pecans pair perfectly with beer and cocktails. Feature these on your next charcuterie board assortment and make sure you have enough for refills!

Preheat the oven to 350°F. Lay the rosemary leaves on a cutting board and roll with a rolling pin to crush. Chop the leaves.

Mix the olive oil, sugar, chopped rosemary, salt, and pepper in a bowl. Add the pecans and toss to coat. Place the pecans on a rimmed baking sheet and roast for 17 to 20 minutes.

GUACAMOLE
ROSEDALE
SUSAN SPICER, CHEF/OWNER

Avocados—delicious, versatile, and good for you—are one of Chef Spicer's favorite foods. At Rosedale, guacamole is made with a minimum of ingredients to let the flavor of the avocado shine through. While it's difficult to find ripe avocados at the grocery store, if you plan ahead and let them sit out at room temperature for a day or two, they will ripen and yield their creamy goodness. Although cilantro is not usually added to Spicer's guacamole (it is sprinkled on top), you can add it in as well. Serve with crispy tortilla chips, and, if you'd like to fully replicate Rosedale's guacamole, sprinkle on Cotija cheese and thinly sliced scallions, too.

In a mixing bowl, mash the avocados with a fork, then add all the other ingredients, except the cilantro (unless you'd like to add some). Taste and adjust seasoning. (The lime and salt should be bright and zingy.) Sprinkle on the cilantro and serve with the tortilla chips.

Note:
The guacamole also is delicious dolloped on grilled fish, steak, or ripe tomatoes.

New Orleans ★

MAKES ABOUT 2 CUPS

4 avocados, ripened

1 jalapeño, stem, seeds, and ribs removed, finely chopped

1 small red onion, finely chopped

3 tablespoons lime juice

1 teaspoon kosher salt, or more to taste

2 tablespoons cilantro, chopped (not too fine), or to taste, for sprinkling

Tortilla chips, for serving

NELLY GONZALES CHAN, *HERITAGE THROUGH FOOD,* OIL/ACRYLIC (DETAIL)

Covington ★

FOR THE PIMENTO CHEESE

1 pound mild shredded cheddar cheese

4 ounces cream cheese, softened

2 red bell peppers, roasted, peeled, and minced

⅛ cup mayonnaise

½ teaspoon kosher salt

1 teaspoon black pepper

½ small onion, minced

3 garlic cloves, minced

½ tablespoon hot sauce

½ tablespoon Lea & Perrins Worcestershire sauce

1 tablespoon red wine vinegar

½ teaspoon dry yellow mustard

PIMENTO CHEESE BRUSCHETTA
LOLA RESTAURANT, COVINGTON
KEITH AND NEALY FRENTZ, CHEFS/OWNERS

Layered roasted red pepper cheese spread, bacon marmalade, and pickled red onions on toasted baguette slices—the dressed-up pimento cheese appetizer by culinary couple Keith and Nealy Frentz—is fit for a king and queen and just the sort of amazing appetizer that brings LOLA patrons back for more. Now you have the recipe to keep guests at your next dinner party reaching for seconds, and thirds, and fourths… Ideally, prepare each element of the dish the day before, so all you'll need to do is assemble and serve.

Make the pimento cheese. In a mixing bowl, combine all ingredients and stir until incorporated. Place in a container and store in the refrigerator.

Make the bacon marmalade. In a pot with a heavy bottom, add the butter, onion, and garlic and let sweat down. Add the bacon and cook for 5 minutes. Add remaining ingredients and continue to cook and reduce until thick and syrupy in texture. (This process takes about 20 to 30 minutes on medium to low heat.) Place in a container and let cool. Store in the refrigerator.

Make the pickled red onion. Combine all ingredients in a pot and boil for 3 minutes. Place in a heatproof container and chill in an ice bath until cool. Store in the refrigerator.

Assemble the bruschetta. When ready to serve, layer the pimento cheese, bacon marmalade, and pickled red onion on top of toasted baguette slices.

MADYSON BERGERON, *TURN UP THE HEAT,* MIXED MEDIA (DETAIL)

FOR THE BACON MARMALADE

½ tablespoon butter

½ yellow onion, diced

2½ cloves garlic, minced

1 pound smoked bacon, diced

1½ tablespoons dried thyme

½ cup sugar

⅛ cup molasses

Zest and juice from half an orange

¼ bottle of red wine

FOR THE PICKLED RED ONION

2 red onions, thinly sliced

3 cloves garlic, minced

2 cups red wine vinegar

½ teaspoon black peppercorns

½ tablespoon mustard seeds

½ tablespoon coriander seeds

½ tablespoon juniper berries

1 bay leaf

½ cup sugar

⅛ cup kosher salt

Toasted baguette slices, for serving

New Iberia

Serves 6

12 strips of your favorite brand of thick-cut smoked bacon

3 cups dark brown sugar

2 cups Cane River Pecan Pieces, or finely chopped Mammoth pecans

PECAN PRALINE BACON
CANE RIVER PECAN COMPANY

Two words: Bacon. Candy. Who wouldn't be interested in trying a delectable combination of thick-cut bacon candied with brown sugar and pecans? Your family and friends will be begging you to bring this to future gatherings. Thankfully, it's fun and easy to make!

Preheat the oven to 320°F. Line the bottom of a baking sheet with aluminum foil. Lay a piece of parchment paper on top of the foil. (If you don't have parchment paper, do not use wax paper because it burns at high temperatures. If you have a silicone baking sheet, you may use that on top of the foil.) Lay out the bacon strips, ¼-inch apart, on the parchment paper. Completely cover each strip of bacon with the brown sugar, then carefully sprinkle the pecan pieces evenly over each strip.

Bake the bacon for 12 minutes, then rotate the baking sheet and cook for another 10 to 15 minutes, until the bacon is bubbling and beginning to get dark brown. (Keep in mind that the bacon will continue to cook while cooling, so be careful not to burn.) Remove the baking sheet from the oven and let it cool to room temperature before removing the bacon. (Be careful when the bacon is first removed, as it is very hot.)

SPINACH, CRAB, AND ARTICHOKE DIP WITH CROSTINI TOASTS

SPAHR'S SEAFOOD
RYAN GAUDET, CHEF

Des Allemands
★

Spinach and artichoke dip is probably the most popular dish at game day parties, and when you follow Chef Gaudet's recipe with Louisiana crabmeat, you've won even before you put it in the oven! Keep this simple recipe in mind for any party, or just any old Louisiana Saturday night!

Make the dip. Melt the butter in a large pot over medium heat, then add the onion and sauté until translucent. Add the flour, whisking until smooth, and cook for about 1 minute. Slowly whisk in the heavy cream, about 1 cup at a time. Add the Cajun seasoning and allow to simmer for about 5 minutes. Add the spinach and artichoke hearts and simmer until the spinach is fully wilted. Add the crabmeat and cheddar and simmer over low to medium heat until cheddar is melted. Remove pot from heat. Scoop some of the dip (amount that you'd like to serve immediately) into a microwave safe dish, then cover the dip with the Parmesan and microwave for 1 minute. (For a crispier topping, place the Parmesan-topped dip in a 400°F oven for 7 minutes.)

Make the crostini toasts. Preheat the oven to 400°F. Spread out the French bread slices on a baking sheet. Season each with the Cajun seasoning, garlic powder, and parsley, then drizzle with the olive oil. Toast in the oven for about 2 minutes, or until golden brown and crispy. Serve the toasts with the dip.

SERVES 4

FOR THE DIP

4 tablespoons unsalted butter, cubed

1 yellow onion, diced

½ cup all-purpose flour

1 quart heavy cream

2 tablespoons Cajun seasoning

1 pound fresh baby spinach, chopped

1 cup artichoke hearts, chopped

8 ounces fresh crabmeat

1 cup grated cheddar cheese

1 cup grated Parmesan cheese

FOR THE CROSTINI TOASTS

1 loaf fresh French bread, sliced thin

1 tablespoon Cajun seasoning

1 tablespoon garlic powder

4 tablespoons chopped parsley

Extra virgin olive oil as needed, for drizzle

CAYDEN LASSEIGNE, *CYPRUS BLUES AND FOODS*, WATERCOLOR

New Orleans
★

SERVES 2 TO 4

½ tablespoon minced garlic

1 tablespoon salted butter

2 to 3 ounces extra virgin olive oil

½ pound Louisiana blue crab fingers

½ teaspoon Cajun seasoning

1 tablespoon freshly squeezed lemon juice

Parmesan cheese, for garnish

2 pinches chopped parsley, for garnish

French bread, cut crostini style, for serving

COCKTAIL CRAB FINGERS
JACK DEMPSEY'S RESTAURANT
SAMMY BAIAMONTE, CHEF/OWNER

This old-school restaurant, housed in a small, white building in the Bywater neighborhood along the Mississippi River levee, isn't named for the famous fighter, but rather a boisterous New Orleans police reporter for the States-Item. First established by a pair of policemen that knew Dempsey well, the restaurant was purchased by Andrew and Diane Marino in 1980. Today, Diane's son, Sammy Baiamonte, and his wife, Desirée, own the restaurant where Sammy has spent much of his adult life preparing and serving a vast array of seafood, along with many family recipes, such as dressings, gumbo, and their famous baked macaroni and cheese. This appetizer is a customer favorite.

In a medium pan, sauté the garlic in the butter and olive oil over medium heat, then add the crab fingers and coat with the mixture. After a minute or two, add the Cajun seasoning and continue to sauté for another minute. While still nice and hot, dish everything onto a serving platter. Squeeze the lemon juice evenly over the fingers. Lightly sprinkle the Parmesan cheese, then the parsley, on top. Dip the bread in the mixture and enjoy!

SARAH KATE KRAMER, *SE RESSAMBLER POUR MANGER,* OIL/ACRYLIC

SHRIMP AND CRABMEAT DIP
VILLAGE CUISINE CATERING AND CAFÉ
RHONDA MEEK, EXECUTIVE CHEF/OWNER

What started thirteen years ago as a small catering business has grown into Village Cuisine Catering and Café—a full-service restaurant and catering company providing delicious, quality meals. And, once a month, don't miss their full-service British Tea Thyme Tuesday!

Drain the shrimp and reserve 2½ tablespoons of shrimp liquid. In a mixer, cream together the cream cheese and reserved shrimp juice. Add the lemon juice, pressed garlic, onion, crabmeat, and half of the shrimp. Add the garlic powder and hot sauce to taste, then add the green onions. Add the rest of the shrimp and fold in carefully. Serve cold with Ritz crackers or warm in a chafing dish.

Note:
The dip will keep in the refrigerator for 1 week and can be frozen.

Grand Cane

2 (4.5-ounce) cans small shrimp

2 (8-ounce) packages cream cheese

4 tablespoons lemon juice

1 tablespoon pressed garlic

1 tablespoon finely diced onion

1 (6.5-ounce) can lump crabmeat, drained

Garlic powder, to taste

Tabasco sauce or LA Hot Sauce, to taste

3 green onions, chopped

Ritz crackers, for serving (optional)

Sulphur

SERVES 3 AS AN APPETIZER

FOR THE WONTONS

5 ounces cream cheese

2 tablespoons minced green onions

1 tablespoon minced shallot

1 teaspoon minced serrano pepper

½ tablespoon minced celery

¼ teaspoon grated fresh ginger

1 teaspoon salt

8 jumbo (21/25) Louisiana shrimp

½ teaspoon Cajun seasoning

½ cup jumbo Louisiana lump crabmeat

15 packaged wonton wrappers

6 cups canola oil, for frying

CRAB AND SHRIMP WONTONS WITH SRIRACHA SWEET CHILI AIOLI
PROSTART/SULPHUR HIGH SCHOOL
JACOB GILLETT, PROSTART EDUCATOR AND CHEF

Wontons come in one shape and size, but the options for fillings and sauces are endless! This crab and shrimp version was created by ProStart Educator Jacob Gillett for his ProStart students to use at the 2022 Raising Cane's Chicken Fingers Louisiana ProStart Invitational. The creamy filling, made with locally caught Gulf crab and shrimp, wowed the judges so much that their appetizer won "Best Starter Award." Drizzle the aioli over the wontons or serve on the side for an extra kick of heat, and you'll have made your very own "Best Starter."

Make the wontons. In a mixing bowl, add the cream cheese, green onions, shallot, serrano pepper, celery, ginger, and salt and mix with a fork until creamy. Mince the shrimp and add the Cajun seasoning. Sift through the crab for shells. Add the shrimp and crab to the cream cheese mixture and stir gently to combine.

Working with one wonton wrapper at a time, wet all 4 edges of the wrapper (this will seal it), then add about 1 tablespoon of the mixture to the middle. Using your fingers, crimp edges together to seal. Continue to fill and seal the remaining wrappers in the same way.

ADDIE RAMER, *HOW WE TRAVEL, MY DAD AND I,* OTHER (DETAIL)

Heat the oil in a 4-quart saucepan until it reaches 350°F degrees, then fry the wontons, in three batches, until golden brown.

Make the aioli. Add the egg yolks, lime juice, rice vinegar, sugar, and pepper to a mixing bowl and whisk together. Slowly drizzle in the canola oil, whisking constantly, until thick. Add the remaining ingredients and mix well.

To serve, place 5 wontons on each plate and either drizzle with the aioli or serve the aioli on the side.

FOR THE SRIRACHA SWEET CHILI AIOLI

2 egg yolks

1 teaspoon lime juice

½ teaspoon rice vinegar

¼ teaspoon granulated sugar

¼ teaspoon black pepper

½ cup canola oil

⅛ teaspoon sesame seed oil

3 tablespoons sweet chili sauce

2 tablespoons sriracha

Darrow ★

SERVES 4

FOR THE CREAM SAUCE

3 cups heavy cream

¼ cup white wine

3 dried bay leaves

Healthy pinch of saffron

Sea salt, to taste

Fresh cracked black
pepper, to taste

1 pound jumbo lump
crabmeat

Green onions, green and
white parts, finely sliced

FOR THE EGGPLANT

10 to 15 cups canola oil,
for frying

6 eggs, beaten

1 cup whole milk

1 medium eggplant, sliced
into ½-inch rounds

Salt and pepper, to taste

6 cups yellow corn flour,
seasoned to taste

EGGPLANT NAPOLEON
HOUMAS HOUSE PLANTATION AND GARDENS
JEREMY LANGLOIS, EXECUTIVE CHEF

Chef Jeremy Langlois leads the culinary team at the Houmas House Plantation and Gardens as Executive Chef of the award-winning Latil's Landing Restaurant, named by Esquire magazine as one of the top twenty best new restaurants in America. There he masterfully creates wonderful dishes in a style that he calls "Nouvelle Louisiane." Using the freshest local ingredients that Louisiana has to offer, Chef Langlois whips up magic in the kitchen and thrives on delivering his guests an unforgettable experience in one of Louisiana's most beautiful settings.

Make the cream sauce. In a large non-reactive pot, add the cream, white wine, bay leaves, saffron, salt, and pepper and simmer gently for about 15 minutes. (It will reduce and thicken a bit during this time. Don't let it boil as it will quickly expand and boil out of the pot.) Once the sauce is seasoned properly, pass through a fine strainer into a clean pot. Add the crabmeat to the sauce and allow to gently simmer while cooking the eggplant.

Cook the eggplant. Heat the oil in a large pot to 350°F. Mix together the eggs and milk. Lightly season the eggplant with salt and pepper, then place in the egg wash. Coat both sides thoroughly then place in the seasoned corn flour and coat both sides. Shake off any excess corn flour and carefully ease into the oil. Gently cook eggplant until the bottom is golden brown, then flip over and cook until other side is golden. Remove from oil and gently pat dry with paper towels.

Add the green onions to the crabmeat and sauce and adjust seasoning, as needed. Place one round of eggplant on a plate, top with some crabmeat and sauce. Place another round on top of the first and top with crabmeat and sauce. Place the final round of eggplant on top and secure with a skewer, then top with sauce. Assemble 3 more Eggplant Napoleons and serve.

BLUE CRAB BEIGNETS
RESTAURANT R'EVOLUTION
JOHN FOLSE, CHEF

Beignets or fritters are extremely common in Southern cuisine, and nothing makes these tasty bites more Louisianian than the addition of lump crabmeat. These beignets make for a perfect party hors d'oeuvre or put three on a plate as an appetizer.

Make the beignet batter. In a medium mixing bowl, mix all the dry ingredients together. Using a wire whisk, whisk in the beer until batter is slightly thicker than pancake batter. Set aside.

Make and fry the crab beignets. In a homestyle deep-fryer such as FryDaddy®, preheat the oil according to manufacturer's directions. If no fryer is available, place 3 inches of the oil in a cast iron Dutch oven and heat to 375°F. In a large mixing bowl, combine the chives, shallot, bell pepper, minced garlic, and mascarpone cheese. Add the lump crabmeat and, using a fork, gently fold into the cheese mixture. Season to taste using salt, black pepper, and granulated garlic. Using your hands, roll crab mixture into ping pong-sized balls or slightly smaller than a golf ball.

One at a time, drop crab balls into prepared beignet batter, lift with a fork to drain off excess batter, then coat in the bread-crumbs. When all the balls are coated, gently drop each ball into fryer and cook, in batches, until crisp and golden brown. Once fried, drain beignets on paper towels. Serve with rémoulade or tartar sauce.

New Orleans

SERVES 16

FOR THE BEIGNET BATTER

1 cup flour

1¼ tablespoons cornstarch

1 tablespoon baking powder

1 cup beer

FOR THE CRAB BEIGNETS

1 quart vegetable oil, for frying

1 tablespoon chopped chives

1 tablespoon minced shallot

¼ cup minced red bell pepper

1 teaspoon minced garlic

3 ounces mascarpone cheese

½ pound fresh lump blue crabmeat

Salt and pepper, to taste

Granulated garlic, to taste

1½ cups seasoned Italian breadcrumbs

Rémoulade or tartar sauce, for serving

Manchac ★

**FOR THE RÉMOULADE
SAUCE**

2 cups mayonnaise

¼ cup ketchup

2 tablespoons Creole
mustard

2 tablespoons horseradish

¼ cup parsley, chopped

¼ cup celery, chopped

¼ cup onions, chopped

CRAWFISH CAKES WITH RÉMOULADE SAUCE
MIDDENDORF'S
HORST PFEIFER, EUROPEAN MASTER CHEF

Middendorf's Crawfish Cakes are one of the old-time favorites at the iconic seafood restaurant. Josie Middendorf created the recipe when Middendorf's began as a small roadside diner back in 1934 in the Manchac, LA swamp. Today, these crawfish cakes often are enjoyed before the delectable Middendorf's World Famous Original Thin Fried Catfish.

Make the sauce. Stir together all the sauce ingredients in a bowl until combined. Cover and set aside in the refrigerator until serving time.

Make the crawfish cakes. Preheat the oven to 350°F. In a bowl, stir together all the ingredients, except the butter, until combined. Shape into 2-ounce patties.

In a skillet, melt the butter over medium heat until browned. Add the crawfish cakes, in batches, and cook until golden brown on both sides, transferring them to a baking sheet as browned. Place the crawfish cakes in the oven for 10 minutes. Serve topped with the rémoulade sauce and garnish as desired.

Be creative with your garnishes. For a great presentation, tilt the crawfish cakes up slightly on shredded lettuce and finish with lemon slices, diced tomatoes, green onions, and jalapeño pepper sauce.

ARIYANA SHIDISKIS, *SERVED UP!,* OIL/ACRYLIC (DETAIL)

FOR THE CRAWFISH CAKES

1 pound crawfish tails, chopped

3 eggs

2 tablespoons mayonnaise

2 tablespoons chopped parsley

2 tablespoons chopped celery

2 tablespoons chopped onion

2 tablespoons chopped green bell pepper

⅔ cup finely chopped stale bread

½ teaspoon Italian seasoning

½ teaspoon Coleman's Mustard Powder

Pinch of garlic salt

Pinch of cumin

4 tablespoons (½ stick) butter

FOR THE GARNISH

Shredded lettuce

Lemon slices

Diced tomato

Chopped green onions

Jalapeño pepper sauce

New Orleans ★

BARBECUE OYSTERS
RED FISH GRILL
RALPH BRENNAN RESTAURANT GROUP
CHRIS VAZQUEZ, CHEF

SERVES 6 AS AN APPETIZER, OR 3 TO 4 AS A MAIN COURSE

FOR THE OYSTERS

Canola oil, for deep frying

2 cups seasoned flour

36 medium-to-large oysters, drained

FOR THE BBQ HOT SAUCE

MAKES ABOUT ½ CUP

¼ cup plus 2 tablespoons mild-flavored Louisiana pepper sauce, such as Crystal

1 tablespoon clover honey

6 tablespoons clarified butter

1 cup Blue Cheese Dipping Sauce (recipe follows), or your favorite blue cheese dressing, for serving

The barbecue oysters are always a hit before any meal at Red Fish Grill. Chef Vazquez uses local Crystal Hot Sauce to turn up the heat on his BBQ sauce. As we all know, the Crystal sauce offers just the right amount of sweet and spice, so the heat never puts the roof of your mouth on fire! Accented with blue cheese dipping sauce to cool it down, the oysters' succulence becomes the star of this appetizer, which has been named a "Most Memorable Meal," according to Forbes.com, and a "Can't Miss Dish," by USA Today.

Heat the oil in a deep fryer to 350°F or heat 1½ to 2 inches of the oil in a 5-quart Dutch oven over medium-high heat to 350°F.

Place the seasoned flour in a large mixing bowl.

Once the oil has almost reached 350°F, drain any excess oyster liquor from a batch of the oysters and dredge them in the seasoned flour.

Carefully slide the oysters, in batches, into the oil. (As the cold oysters come in contact with the hot oil, it may momentarily bubble up in the pan.) Fry the oysters just until golden brown and crispy, about two minutes. Remove the finished oysters from the oil with a slotted spoon and drain on paper towels. Continue to dredge, fry, and drain the remaining oysters in batches.

As soon as all the fried oysters have been drained, add small batches of them to the bowl of BBQ Hot Sauce and toss to coat well. Serve while still warm with the Blue Cheese Dipping Sauce.

BBQ HOT SAUCE

Combine the pepper sauce and honey in a blender. Set aside.

In a very small saucepan over medium heat, warm the clarified butter to 140°F, using a frying thermometer to access temperature. You may also heat the butter in a microwave oven in a small microwaveable bowl. (If you just prepared the clarified

ANNA MILEY, *AWE SHUCKS,* OTHER (SECOND PLACE JUNIOR)

butter and it's still over 140°F, you don't need to cool it down.)

Promptly turn the blender to low speed and slowly pour the 140°F butter in a thin steady stream through the hole in the blender's lid. Pour barbecue sauce into a large, nonreactive mixing bowl and set aside.

BLUE CHEESE DIPPING SAUCE

Combine all the ingredients in a medium mixing bowl and blend well with a whisk. The blue cheese dipping sauce may be passed at the table or served on the plates with the oysters.

FOR THE BLUE CHEESE DIPPING SAUCE

MAKES ABOUT 1½ CUPS

4 ounces blue cheese, crumbled

¾ cup mayonnaise

2 tablespoons buttermilk

1 tablespoon distilled white vinegar

1½ tablespoons vegetable oil

1 tablespoon minced flat-leaf parsley

⅛ teaspoon kosher salt

⅛ teaspoon freshly ground black pepper

SALMON SALTINES
CITY PORK BRASSERIE & BAR
SCOTT DARDENNE, CHEF

Baton Rouge ★

Charcuterie boards are so much fun. With all the crackers, cheeses, nuts, jams, and meats laid out, they truly can be picture perfect. And then, you dig in! When creating your next board, switch it up and add smoked salmon and dill aioli. Chef Scott Dardenne preps this dish multiple times a night. It's a hit with diners at all City Pork locations. Just like on the big game day, Chef Dardenne knows how to prep his kitchen staff for a successful dinner service. Appetizers and charcuterie boards alike!

On a small charcuterie board, arrange the salmon in the center. Place the saltines off to one side. On one side of the salmon, place the pickled onion; on the other, place the raw onion. Place the dill aioli in a silver ramekin and arrange on the far corner from the crackers. In the remaining open space, gently fan the avocado slices as neatly as possible. Use the sundried tomato and caper relish to fill any remaining empty space on the board.

SERVES 4

4-ounce portion of smoked salmon

8 saltines (or lavash crackers)

1 ounce pickled red onion

1 red onion, julienned

2 ounces dill aioli

¼ large avocado, sliced

2 ounces sundried tomato and caper relish

CALLAN THORNTON, *FRESHER THAN EXPECTED*, OTHER (FIRST PLACE SENIOR)

Lafayette

BAYOU BALLS
W. D. & MARY BAKER SMITH CAREER CENTER
KANDICE DEQUEANT, PROSTART EDUCATOR

MAKES 3 CROQUETTES

½ cup minced alligator meat

⅛ cup minced large oysters

½ teaspoon minced green onion

½ teaspoon minced red onion

½ teaspoon minced celery

½ teaspoon minced garlic

¼ teaspoon minced fresh thyme leaves

¾ teaspoon kosher salt

¾ teaspoon black pepper

3 large eggs, divided

2 tablespoons milk

1 tablespoon butter

½ cup plus 1 tablespoon flour, divided

2 tablespoons chicken stock

1 tablespoon heavy cream

1 teaspoon lemon juice

¾ teaspoon cayenne pepper

¾ teaspoon garlic powder

½ cup Italian seasoned breadcrumbs

The W.D. & Mary Baker Smith Career Center in Lafayette offers juniors and seniors the opportunity to take a ProStart class to prepare them for a future job in the culinary and hospitality fields. Under the direction of educator Kandice Dequeant, students learn lessons on sanitation and safety, knife skills, and recipe basics. This delightful recipe, with its many ingredients, puts her students through their paces!

In a mixing bowl, gently combine the alligator meat, oysters, green and red onions, celery, garlic, and thyme. Season the alligator mixture with the salt and pepper and set aside.

Separate a yolk from one egg and place in a small bowl. Mix in the milk and set the mixture aside.

In a medium pan, melt the butter over medium heat. Stir in 1 tablespoon of the flour until absorbed. Slowly stir in the chicken stock and then the cream, stirring until a thick Béchamel sauce is formed.

Stir the reserved alligator mixture into the Béchamel sauce along with the lemon juice, cayenne pepper, and garlic powder. Remove pan from the heat and fold in the reserved yolk mixture. Stir to incorporate and return to the heat, stirring until heated thoroughly and very creamy. Taste and adjust seasonings as needed. Remove the croquette mixture from the heat and pour into a dish to cool. Cover and refrigerate (or put in the freezer for 30 minutes) to cool completely.

While the croquette mixture is cooling, prepare individual bowls for coating the croquette balls, after they are formed, as follows: a bowl for the remaining 2 eggs (beaten), a bowl for the breadcrumbs, and another bowl for the panko.

When the croquette mixture is cooled completely and you are ready to form and fry the croquettes, heat the oil to 350°F in a deep-frying pan or small pot. Using a portion scoop, gather and form the croquette mixture into a 2-ounce ball (about the size of a golf ball). Dust heavily with enough of the remaining flour to keep from becoming too sticky, then add enough additional flour to make a well-formed ball that will hold together while frying. Make more balls in the same manner with the remaining mixture.

Now you are ready to coat the balls and fry them. Roll 1 ball lightly in the beaten egg mixture, then cover well with the seasoned breadcrumbs, and then the plain panko. Coat the remaining balls in the same way. Fry the balls in the hot oil (completely submerged) over medium heat until delicate brown and cooked through. Drain on paper towels. To serve, plate the croquettes. Garnish with parsley and serve with aioli.

½ cup plain panko breadcrumbs

2 cups vegetable oil, for frying

½ teaspoon chopped parsley, for garnish

Aioli, for serving

NICHOLAS HOWARD, *GALETTE DES ROIS EN FORME D'ALLIGATOR, OTHER*

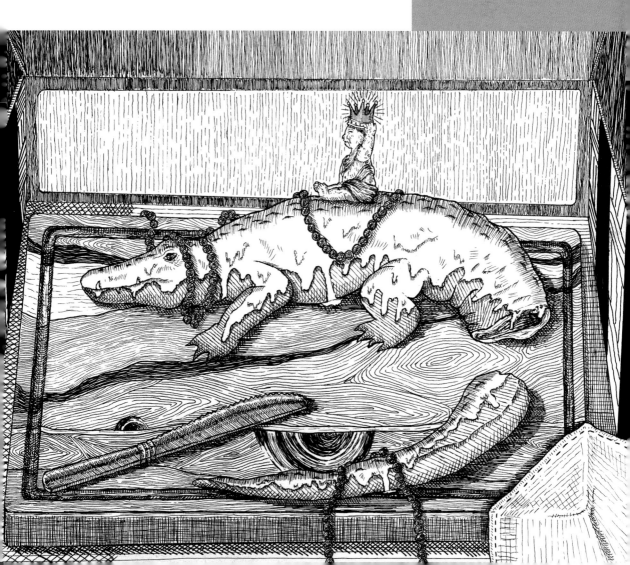

Des Allemands ★

MAKES 6 CAKES

1 tablespoon liquid crab boil

2 pounds wild-caught Louisiana catfish

1 cup mayonnaise

2 tablespoons Creole mustard

2 tablespoons Cajun seasoning

1 cup breadcrumbs

¼ cup (½ stick) butter

½ cup small-diced bell pepper

½ cup small-diced onion

¼ cup small-diced celery

1 tablespoon olive oil

CATFISH CAKES
SPAHR'S SEAFOOD RESTAURANTS
DONALD SPAHR, OWNER

You'll find a truly authentic Cajun dining experience at Spahr's Seafood. Back in 1968, founder Bill Spahr Jr. created the restaurant in his hometown of Des Allemands. He passed in late 2021, leaving his legacy of Cajun cuisine and warm hospitality to his family, and today his grandson Donald owns the establishment that once served as a service station for fisherman along the Bayou. Over the years, Spahr's turned into a full-service restaurant and opened additional locations in Galliano and Thibodaux. Known for using only fresh-caught seafood in simple ways (like the thick, plump catfish used in this take on a crab cake), Chef Donald brings his passion for fishing and seafood to his culinary techniques. Here the Cajun "holy trinity" of bell pepper, onion, and celery plays a major role.

Preheat the oven to 350°F if you would like to finish off the fish cakes in the oven. In a large pot of boiling water, add the liquid crab boil, then boil the catfish for 6 minutes. Drain the fish and let cool.

Once cool, flake the fish apart into a large mixing bowl. Add the mayonnaise, Creole mustard, Cajun seasoning, and breadcrumbs and stir to combine.

In a saucepan, melt the butter, then add the bell pepper, onion, and celery and sauté until soft. Add vegetables to the fish mixture and stir gently to combine. Form into cakes.

Add the oil to a pan or flattop and grill fish cakes 3 to 4 minutes on each side, until golden brown and crispy on the edges. (Or deep fry in a deep pan with more oil until golden brown and crispy.) If desired, transfer to a baking sheet and finish in the oven for 5 minutes.

Note:
If you prefer, the catfish cakes can be served as a main dish. There are enough cakes for 2 people.

MINI MUFFULETTAS
P-BEAU'S QUALITY FOOD & DRINK
PETER SCLAFANI, CHEF

Muffulettas are high on the list of Louisiana comfort foods. Story has it, these Italian-style sandwiches were created by Salvatore Lupo, a Sicilian immigrant, who opened Central Grocery in 1906. The muffuletta itself was invented in the early 20th century to feed the Sicilian and Italian truck drivers who were delivering produce to the French Market. These bite-sized sammies pack a punch and wipe out hunger just as good as a full-size version. Serve these at your next game day party for instantly happy guests!

Make the olive salad. Combine all ingredients in a food processor. Pulse several times to get a course consistency. Store in an airtight container.

Make the muffulettas. On the sliced Italian rolls, place the sliced ham, Genoa salami, provolone cheese, mortadella, and olive salad. The key to a good muffuletta is to let the bread soak up the seasoned olive oil from the olive salad. It is not traditional, but muffulettas can be warmed in the oven.

Note:
The olive salad will keep in the refrigerator for 2 weeks.

Denham Springs

MAKES 24 MINI
MUFFULETTAS

FOR THE OLIVE SALAD

1 cup black olives, pitted

1 cup green olives, pitted

¼ cup chopped red onions

¼ cup chopped celery

2 tablespoons chopped garlic

¼ cup chopped green onions

¼ cup chopped Italian parsley

1 tablespoon oregano

1 cup extra virgin olive oil

¼ cup red wine vinegar

1 teaspoon freshly ground black pepper

FOR THE MUFFULETTAS

24 small Italian rolls (with sesame seeds, optional)

24 slices ham

24 slices Genoa salami

24 slices provolone cheese

6 slices mortadella, cut into quarters

MAKES 12 MUFFINS

FOR THE CORNBREAD

½ pound (2 sticks) unsalted butter, softened

1 cup light brown sugar

2 tablespoons melted butter, plus more for greasing muffin wells

1¼ cups small-diced fresh pineapple

2 eggs

¼ cup plus 3 tablespoons vegetable oil

2 tablespoons heavy cream

2 tablespoons buttermilk

2½ tablespoons honey

1 tablespoon dark Karo syrup

1⅓ cups all-purpose flour

½ cup plus 1½ tablespoons yellow cornmeal

⅓ cup sugar

1 tablespoon baking powder

¾ teaspoon salt

PINEAPPLE UPSIDE-DOWN CORNBREAD WITH BACON MARMALADE
MERIL
EMERIL LAGASSE, OWNER/CHEF

Cornbread has long been a Cajun-Creole staple, and the pineapple upside down cake has a history that goes back just as far. Before ovens were made reliable for baking, cast iron skillets were the host for cake baking and, to turn cakes nice and sweet, people would fill the bottom of the skillet with local fruit. Flipping was easy with the durability of the cast iron handle. Chef Emeril Lagasse's intuitional palate and his love for food and Southern hospitality have made him one of the biggest global culinary names, especially in New Orleans. He operates his home base here with his team of chefs creating and testing recipes in the Warehouse District. These amazing muffins, served at his restaurant Meril, are a modern take on the classic "skillet cake." You'll love playing Chef in the kitchen with this recipe. BAM! Your tasty snack is ready.

Preheat the oven to 400°F. In a mixing bowl, combine the softened butter and light brown sugar and, using a pastry blender or two forks, blend to a uniform consistency.

Butter the wells of a standard size muffin pan with some of the melted butter, then divide the pineapple evenly among the 12 wells. Using a small scoop or a tablespoon as a guide, divide the butter and brown sugar mixture evenly among the wells.

Transfer to the oven and bake for 15 minutes. Remove pan from the oven and allow to cool to room temperature before proceeding with the recipe.

Once the muffin pan has cooled, combine the eggs, oil, ½ cup of water, heavy cream, buttermilk and 2 tablespoons melted butter in a mixing bowl and whisk to blend. Stir in the honey and Karo until blended.

Combine the flour, cornmeal, sugar, baking powder, and salt in a mixing bowl and whisk to blend. Stir in the liquid ingredients just until the dry ingredients are moistened.

Place about ¼ cup of the cornmeal batter into each of 12 muffin wells on top of the butter-pineapple mixture. (You will have a bit of batter leftover; you can bake it in two additional muffin cups or in a small pan, as desired.) Place the muffin tin on a sheet pan (in case the muffins bubble over during baking) and bake the muffins until golden brown and cooked through, 15 to 18 minutes.

Remove from the oven and let cool briefly, then run a thin knife around the edge of the muffins and turn them out onto a serving plate. Serve the upside-down cornbread muffins warm, with the Bacon Marmalade, if desired.

HOUSE-CURED BACON MARMALADE

In a large skillet, fry the bacon over medium-low heat until crispy and fat is completely rendered, 25 to 30 minutes. Drain bacon from fat (save drippings for another purpose) and place bacon on paper towels to drain. Once cooled, finely chop the bacon and set aside.

In a 2-quart heavy sauce pot, combine the vinegar, brown sugar, garlic, chili powder, and paprika and boil until you see nickel-size bubbles breaking across the top.

Make a slurry with the pectin, 2 tablespoons of water, the sugar, and 1 teaspoon of the calcium water made from the packet that comes with the pectin. Stir this slurry into the jam until thickened and blended.

Stir in the bacon and set aside to cool. If jam seems too thick, once it has cooled, you can add a bit of water to thin it.

Note:
We used Pomona's Universal Pectin, which comes in powdered form in an envelope in a small box, along with a packet of monocalcium phosphate that is mixed with water to activate the pectin. If you cannot find this in your area, you could use a small amount of liquid pectin, or you can simply skip the pectin, and just add the 4 teaspoons of sugar dissolved in the 2 tablespoons water. In that case, the marmalade will have a slightly looser texture, but it still works fine as a spread for the muffins.

FOR THE HOUSE-CURED BACON MARMALADE

MAKES ABOUT 2 CUPS

1 pound house-cured bacon (or your favorite thick-cut cured and smoked bacon), cut into small dice

1 cup Steen's cane vinegar

1 cup light brown sugar

2 tablespoons minced garlic

4 teaspoons chili powder

4 teaspoons smoked paprika

1 teaspoon pectin (see Note below)

4 teaspoons sugar

CHAPTER TWO
SOUPS AND SALADS

New Iberia

SERVES 8 TO 10

1 sack (40 pounds)
live crawfish

3 large onions,
finely chopped

2 medium bell peppers,
finely chopped

2 celery ribs, finely
chopped

2½ to 3 cups peanut
butter-colored roux

1 tablespoon salt

2 teaspoons ground
white pepper

1 teaspoon ground
red pepper

1 teaspoon ground
black pepper

1 cup chopped
green onions

½ cup chopped parsley

CRAWFISH BISQUE
ALEX PATOUT, CHEF

For this dish, the saying goes, you need either three days or two families–large Cajun families. One good time to make it is after you've had a big crawfish boil and have all those nice, peeled tails ready to go. You may end up with leftover bisque, but it will be delicious, and you'll have discovered the ecstasy of a week-long crawfish binge.

Fill a large (8-gallon) stockpot with water, one-third full, and bring to a heavy boil over high heat. If you have a large wire basket, place the crawfish in the basket or simply pour the crawfish into the pot and cook, covered. As soon as steam begins to escape from under the lid, turn the heat off and remove the crawfish. Spread them on a large surface covered with paper and let cool.

When the crawfish are cool enough to handle, separate the heads and claws from the tails. Using a small spoon or your finger, remove the "fat" from the heads and reserve it in a bowl. Reach inside the heads to remove the mud pockets from between the eyes and discard. Place the claws and three quarters of the heads in a 6- to 8-quart stockpot and add water to cover. Bring to a boil and let boil over medium heat for about an hour. Strain the stock into a clean stockpot and let it cool. Discard the claws and heads.

While the stock is boiling, peel the crawfish tails. Discard the peels and reserve the tails.

Prepare the Stuffed Heads (see procedure opposite).

Return the crawfish stock to a boil over medium-high heat and add the onions, bell peppers, and celery. Reduce the heat and let simmer 15 to 20 minutes. Stir in just enough roux to make a mixture thicker than a soup but thinner than a typical gumbo (don't think of "bisque" in the usual sense). Stir in three-quarters of the reserved crawfish fat and the salt and peppers and let simmer for 45 minutes to 1 hour. (The bisque can be prepared in advance to this point and stored in the refrigerator, where it will keep well for 2 to 3 days.)

About 20 minutes before serving, return the bisque to a simmer, add the remaining crawfish tails (those not used in the Stuffed Heads), and let simmer for 5 minutes. Add the Stuffed

Heads, return to a boil, and let simmer for 15 minutes. Stir in the green onions and parsley and remove from the heat. Serve immediately, distributing the heads and tails evenly among the bowls.

THE STUFFED HEADS

Chop the crawfish tails medium fine and reserve. Melt the butter in a Dutch oven or other large heavy pot over medium-high heat and add the onions, bell peppers, and celery. Sauté, stirring often, until very soft, 30 to 40 minutes. Add the salt and peppers and cook 5 to 7 minutes more. Stir in the crawfish fat and cook for another 10 minutes. Add the chopped crawfish tails, reduce heat to medium, and cook 10 to 15 minutes more. Remove from heat and stir in the breadcrumbs to make a very stiff dressing. Stir in the green onions, parsley, and Tabasco sauce, transfer to a separate container, and let cool. (The dressing can be prepared 2 to 3 days in advance and stored in the refrigerator. If you want to stuff the heads immediately, you can accelerate the cooking process by placing the hot dressing directly in the refrigerator and stirring it every 30 minutes until completely cooled.)

To stuff the heads: Hold a crawfish head in one hand. With the other hand, using a spoon or your fingers, stuff the cavity, packing the dressing so that it does not protrude beyond the shell. Place the flour in a flat pan and roll the heads in it lengthwise so that both the exposed ends are coated, but not the entire shell. (Too much flour on the heads will make the bisque too thick). Place the stuffed heads on cookie sheets, dressing side up, as you finish them. (This whole process goes a lot faster with a three- or four-person assembly line).

Preheat the oven to 375°F. Bake the heads for 20 minutes, then place them under the broiler for 3 to 4 minutes to brown the tops. Transfer the heads to a separate container and let them cool.

Note:
The heads can be prepared 2 to 3 days in advance.

FOR THE STUFFED HEADS

Half of the cooked, peeled crawfish tails from Crawfish Bisque

2 cups (1 pound) butter

5 large onions, finely chopped

4 large bell peppers, finely chopped

3 celery ribs, finely chopped

1 tablespoon salt

2 teaspoons ground red pepper

1 teaspoon ground black pepper

1 teaspoon ground white pepper

Remaining quarter of the crawfish fat from bisque

2 cups breadcrumbs

½ cup chopped green onions

½ cup chopped parsley

Tabasco sauce, to taste

One-quarter of the cooked, cooled crawfish heads from bisque

Flour for dredging (about 2 cups)

New Orleans ★

SERVES 4 TO 6

FOR THE SEASONING MIX

2 teaspoons kosher salt

1 teaspoon each: cayenne pepper, ground white pepper, dried thyme, ground dry mustard

½ teaspoon freshly ground black pepper

½ teaspoon dried basil

FOR THE SOUP STOCK

2 pounds medium to large Louisiana shrimp, shells on

4 ears fresh corn, shucked

1 medium onion

2 to 3 stalks celery

1 small green bell pepper

2 glasses white wine (plus 1 for you)

¼ cup vegetable oil

¼ cup all-purpose flour

1 tablespoon minced fresh garlic (2 to 3 cloves)

4 tablespoons unsalted butter

1 bunch scallions (green parts only), thinly sliced, for garnish

SHRIMP AND CORN SOUP
NEW ORLEANS CULINARY & HOSPITALITY INSTITUTE (NOCHI)
PHILIPE LAMANCUSA, EVENTS CHEF

Fresh Gulf shrimp are the backbone of this simple, yet elegant, crowd pleaser of a soup. Instead of using a pre-made or store-bought stock, you'll resourcefully make your own by using the shrimp shells and vegetable scraps to deeply infuse the soup with flavor. This is best with fresh, sweet summer corn. Just be sure not to waste the corn "milk," which enriches the soup without adding any extra dairy, by scraping the cobs over your pot! That said, if fresh corn on the cob is not available, anything you can find year-round—even frozen kernels—works fine.

Make the seasoning mix. In a small bowl, combine all the seasoning ingredients and set aside.

(Sip your wine.)

Prepare the ingredients for the stock. Gather all your ingredients before starting and lay them out in front of you (this is your *mise en place*). Working over a large stockpot, peel the shrimp, allowing the shells to drop into the pot. Set aside the peeled shrimp. Cut the kernels from the corn cobs and finely dice the onion, celery, and bell pepper; as you work, throw the scraps (corn cobs, onion peels, etc.) into the stockpot. Set aside the vegetables. (You should have approximately 3 cups corn kernels, 1 cup diced onion, ¾ cup diced celery, and ½ cup diced bell pepper.)

Make the stock. Fill the stockpot containing the shrimp shells and scraps, about two-thirds full, with cold water and 2 glasses of wine, and bring to a simmer over medium heat. Let simmer gently for 30 to 45 minutes, or until deeply flavored and reduced a bit. Strain the stock into another pot and discard the solids. You should have 6 to 8 cups of stock; if you have less, top it off with water.

While the stock simmers, make the roux. In another heavy-bottomed pot over medium-high heat, add the vegetable oil. Once the oil is shimmering, reduce the heat to medium and add the flour slowly, stirring with each addition, until incorporated. Cook, stirring frequently, until it is the color of peanut butter.

Add the chopped onions to the roux and stir to incorporate (this will also stop the roux from cooking any further). Fold in the celery, bell pepper, and garlic and cook for about 5 minutes, until translucent. Season the vegetables with about half of the seasoning mix (save the rest for finishing). Add the shrimp and stir for a minute or two, just until slightly pink.

Pour in 6 cups of the strained stock along with the corn kernels. Cook over medium-low heat for about 30 minutes, until it starts to thicken just a bit. If you prefer your soup a bit thinner, add more of the strained stock, as needed.

Remove the pot from the heat and immediately stir in the butter, allowing it to melt completely.

Serve the soup in heated bowls, garnished with the sliced scallions. Sprinkle with some of the remaining seasoning mix to taste. Voilà!

GEORGIA REYNOLDS, *THE CIRCLE OF CAJUN LIFE,* MIXED MEDIA

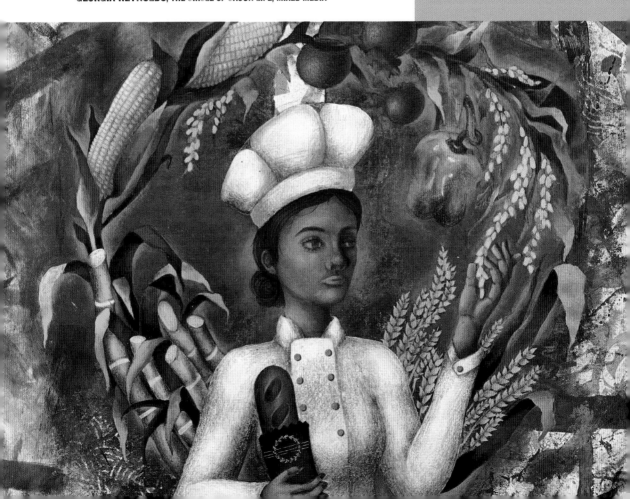

Baton Rouge ★

SERVES 6

½ cup olive oil

1 cup chopped
yellow onion

1 cup chopped leeks

4 cloves garlic, smashed

3 large ripe tomatoes,
chopped

2½ quarts seafood stock

1 tablespoon fresh thyme

1 tablespoon chopped
parsley

1 tablespoon chopped
basil

2 tablespoons orange zest

½ teaspoon saffron
threads

1 tablespoon kosher
salt, plus additional for
seasoning, if needed

1 pound (16/20) shrimp,
peeled

1 pound redfish, cubed

1 pound mussels

Freshly ground black
pepper, to taste

BOUILLABAISSE
ROUJ CREOLE
NOAH LESSARD, CHEF

Sitting inside of Perkins Rowe in Baton Rouge is Rouj Creole of City Group Hospitality. Rouj Creole features menu items that are a mix of the most covetable dishes from around the world, with a Creole flare. This recipe for bouillabaisse highlights the natural flavors of Louisiana seafood with citrus and herbs. Chef Noah Lessard brings together shrimp, redfish, and mussels for a bouillabaisse you'll want to make over and over again.

Heat the oil in a tall pot (8-quart stockpot) over medium heat. Add the onion and leeks and cook gently until softened. Stir in the garlic and cook for a minute until fragrant, then add the tomatoes, stock, herbs, orange zest, saffron, and salt. Bring to a simmer, then reduce the heat so that the broth bubbles slowly without boiling. Cook 30 minutes, then strain the broth into a large bowl or another pot and discard the solids.

Pour the broth back into the stockpot and bring it to a boil. Add the shrimp and cook until they turn pink. Add the fish and mussels, cover, and simmer until the mussels open, 3 to 4 minutes. Taste the soup and add salt or pepper, if needed.

NOTHING IS MISSING

People love inside
cause the change starts within
Be okay where you reside cause the time comes within
and there will be many days
where you fight to know what missing

What's missing, I feel the back row missing
That feeling that you get when diamonds and gold glisten
That feel walking on water grow smarter, work harder, build passion, no passing, on positive
naturals, no fashion
The back row is better, the cheese of the cheddar, the bass of the drum, the blue of the sky, the
cape with the fly, the paper with cash, to live life fast just kicking your feet up, aint no thought
of a re-up, just living life large

People love inside
cause the change starts within
Be okay where you reside cause the time comes within
and there will be many days
where you fight to know what missing

What's missing, I feel the front row missing, that camera that detects what's gonna hurt you if
you don't listen.
I know the things that we fear are the things that we don't know, the front row detects this and
tells us to go, The reason we fight light and when we fight light we get right and fall with no sight.

People love inside
cause the change starts within
Be okay where you reside cause the time comes within
and there will be many days
where you fight to know what missing

KALEB SUMMERS, NOTHING IS MISSING, FIRST PLACE WINNER - SONGWRITING CONTEST,
NEW ORLEANS CENTER FOR CREATIVE ARTS, NEW ORLEANS

New Orleans ★

GULF CIOPPINO
GW FINS
MICHAEL NELSON, EXECUTIVE CHEF
GARY WOLLERMAN, OWNER

SERVES 8 TO 10

2 pounds Louisiana shrimp, shell-on

1 whole 2-pound fish

1 pound fresh crabmeat

½ cup finely diced salt cod

¼ cup extra virgin olive oil

1 cup finely diced onions

1 cup finely diced fennel

1 tablespoon finely diced shallot

2 tablespoons thinly sliced garlic

½ teaspoon dried oregano

¼ teaspoon red pepper flakes

2 teaspoons Creole seasoning

2 teaspoons Old Bay® Seafood Seasoning

½ teaspoon garlic powder

½ teaspoon onion powder

⅛ teaspoon black pepper

1 tablespoon tomato paste

⅓ cup white wine

4 cups tomatoes, crushed

16 ounces clam juice

⅓ cup julienned basil

French bread and Parmesan cheese, for serving

Known for his revolutionary butchering technique ("ocean conservation cuts," as he calls them), Chef Nelson utilizes every aspect of Gulf seafood, as well as pristine fish from all corners of the globe, in his remarkable GW Fins dishes. When possible, he even works with spearfish divers to bring in their morning catch for the chefs to prepare and offer on that evening's dinner menu. Using seasonal ingredients and subtle culinary techniques, the individual flavor and texture of each variety of fish is showcased in elegant simplicity.

Pro tip: Chef Paul Prudhomme's Seafood Magic is the preferred Creole seasoning for this dish.

Prepare the fish and shellfish: Peel and devein the shrimp, reserving the shells. Fillet and skin the whole fish, reserving the bones and skin, then cut the flesh into 1-inch dice. Pick over the crabmeat, discarding any shells. Rinse the finely diced salt cod under cold running water for 10 minutes. Set aside.

Prepare the seafood stock. In a large pot, place the reserved shrimp shells, fish bones, and skin. Barely cover with water and bring to a boil. Turn off the heat. Strain the stock into a large bowl, discarding shells, bones, and skin. Reserve to finish the soup.

Heat the oil in a large pot, then add the onions and sweat for 5 minutes. Add the fennel and cook until soft, about 15 minutes. When the onions are soft, add the shallot, garlic, and salt cod and cook 5 minutes more. Stir in the spices and tomato paste and cook for 3 minutes. Deglaze the pot with the white wine and briefly cook out the alcohol. Add the tomatoes and clam juice and simmer for 30 minutes on low heat. Stir in the fresh basil. (If desired, this part of the recipe can be made ahead and refrigerated.)

To finish the Cioppino, add enough of the strained seafood stock (2-4 cups) to thin to the desired consistency. Add the prepared fish, shrimp, and crab, bring to a simmer, and gently cook for 15 to 20 minutes. Serve with crusty French bread and freshly grated Parmesan cheese.

CREOLE SNAPPING TURTLE SOUP

RESTAURANT R'EVOLUTION
JOHN FOLSE, CHEF

New Orleans

There's been much debate as to whether restaurants should feature turtle soup, due to the endangered species issue surrounding sea turtles. However, in Louisiana, turtle soups, such as this one, are made with snapper. This delicious meat arguably makes the best and most sought-after turtle soup in the world.

Season the turtle meat well with the salt and cayenne pepper. In a heavy-bottomed stockpot, heat ¼ cup of the vegetable oil over medium-high heat. Add the turtle meat and pan-fry until liquid has evaporated and the meat is caramelized and golden brown. Remove meat, drain on paper towels, then set aside.

Remove any remaining liquid from the pot, then heat the remaining ½ cup vegetable oil over medium-high heat. Whisk in the flour, stirring constantly until a dark brown roux is achieved. Add the onions, celery, bell peppers, and garlic and sauté 3 to 5 minutes, or until vegetables are wilted. Stir in the tomato sauce and cook 2 to 3 additional minutes. Slowly add the beef stock, one ladle at a time, stirring constantly until it reaches a soup-like consistency.

Return the browned turtle meat to the pot, add the lemon slices, and season lightly using salt, cayenne pepper, and hot sauce. Bring soup to a rolling boil, then reduce heat to a simmer and cook approximately 45 minutes, or until turtle is fork tender. Add the green onions, parsley, nutmeg, cloves, and cinnamon and cook 2 to 3 minutes more. Adjust seasonings if necessary. When ready to serve, ladle a generous portion of soup into each serving bowl and garnish with 3 deviled quail egg halves. Gently pour ½ ounce of Madeira over each bowl of soup and enjoy.

SERVES 6

2 pounds ground snapping turtle meat

Salt and cayenne pepper, to taste

¾ cup vegetable oil, divided

1 cup flour

2 cups diced onions

1 cup diced celery

1 cup diced green bell peppers

¼ cup minced garlic

2 (8-ounce) cans tomato sauce

3 quarts beef stock

1 lemon, sliced

Louisiana hot sauce, to taste

½ cup sliced green onions

¼ cup chopped parsley

¼ teaspoon ground nutmeg

¼ teaspoon ground cloves

Pinch of ground cinnamon

18 deviled quail egg halves, for garnish

3 ounces Madeira, for topping

New Orleans ★

ALLIGATOR SOUP
JACK ROSE
BRIAN LANDRY, CHEF/OWNER

Growing up in New Orleans, Brian Landry spent a lot of time fishing, therefore gaining a natural love for seafood and cooking. His alligator soup pays homage to those roots. Today, he oversees his QED Hospitality group with restaurants in New Orleans and Nashville. Jack Rose, located in the historic Pontchartrain Hotel, has been open since 2018.

Season the alligator meat with all the dry spices. Heat the oil in a large soup pot over high heat, then add the alligator meat and sear, stirring until browned. Lower the heat to medium, add the onions, celery, bell pepper, and garlic, and cook until browned, stirring constantly to ensure that nothing scorches on the bottom of the pan Add the bay leaves, then gradually add the flour, stirring until the flour is completely incorporated and there are no lumps. Gradually stir in the sherry, red wine, shrimp stock, and chicken stock. Add the crushed tomatoes, thyme, oregano, and basil, stirring to combine, and bring to a boil. Lower the heat to medium and simmer, covered, for an hour.

Skim any excess oil from the top of the soup. Add the lemon zest and juice, minced eggs, and parsley. Check the seasoning and add the Tabasco sauce, salt, and pepper to taste. Serve and enjoy.

SERVES 10 TO 12

2½ pounds ground alligator meat

1 tablespoon kosher salt

1 teaspoon black pepper

2 teaspoons smoked paprika

½ teaspoon chili powder

½ teaspoon crushed red pepper flakes

½ teaspoon ground allspice

½ teaspoon ground coriander

¼ teaspoon ground clove

¼ teaspoon cumin

¼ cup olive oil

2 medium yellow onions, finely diced

2 stalks celery, finely diced

1 green bell pepper, finely diced

4 cloves garlic, minced

CHANDLER VEDROS, *CAJUN'S LENT*, MIXED MEDIA (DETAIL)

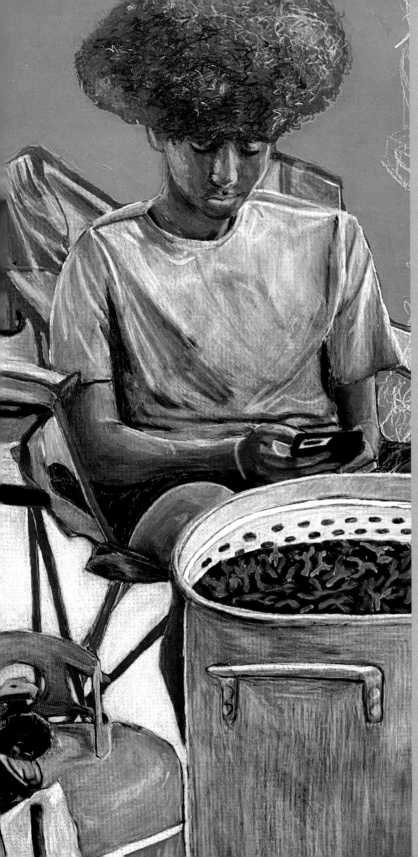

2 bay leaves

½ cup all-purpose flour

1 cup dry sherry

1 cup red wine

3 cups shrimp stock

3 cups chicken stock

1 cup crushed canned tomatoes

1 sprig thyme, picked

1 sprig oregano, picked

2 sprigs basil, chopped

2 lemons, zested and juiced

3 hard boiled eggs, minced

1 bunch parsley, finely chopped

Tabasco sauce, to taste

Salt and black pepper, to taste

New Orleans ★

MAKES 30 CUPS

Canola oil, for cooking

1 cup diced onion

½ cup diced green
bell pepper

½ cup diced celery

1 cup diced carrots

¼ cup minced garlic

1 tablespoon dried thyme

2 tablespoons dried basil

1 teaspoon crushed
red pepper

4 cups diced mirliton
(½-inch dice)

1 pound alligator sausage,
cut into half-moon slices

1 cup tomato paste

1½ gallons shrimp stock

2 cups diced potatoes
(½-inch dice)

Cajun seasoning, to taste

Salt and pepper, to taste

1 pound (31/35) shrimp

Cilantro, for garnish

NEW ORLEANS MIRLITON, SHRIMP, AND ALLIGATOR CHOWDER
SHERATON NEW ORLEANS HOTEL
DARREN HARPER, CHEF

Southerners love mirliton. Better known as chayote in other parts of the world, this particular squash is mostly paired with seafood and enjoyed around the Thanksgiving and Christmas holidays. During that time of the year, rich stuffing dishes, au gratins, and stews are made as side dishes for holiday dinners. With this recipe, Chef Harper decided to do a spin on Manhattan clam chowder. The alligator sausage and mirliton are local products. This soup is so flavorful, it should be enjoyed year-round.

Heat a two-gallon stockpot over medium heat, then add the canola oil. When the oil is hot, add the onion, green bell pepper, celery, carrots, garlic, thyme, basil, crushed red pepper, mirliton, and alligator sausage and sauté for about 6 minutes. Stir in the tomato paste evenly, then pour in the stock and simmer for 20 minutes.

Add the potatoes and seasonings and simmer 10 more minutes. Taste and adjust seasoning if necessary.

Add the shrimp and simmer for 3 more minutes. Remove pot from the heat. To serve, garnish the chowder with cilantro (leaves or chopped).

CREOLE TOMATO SOUP
PHIL'S OYSTER BAR
PETER SCLAFANI, CHEF

Baton Rouge

Tomato soup is a simple dish best served with a grilled cheese sandwich, so make sure to have one ready to eat with this warm bowl of Creole Tomato Soup from Phil's Oyster bar. San Marzano tomatoes make this recipe extra tasty, as they are the cream of the crop of Italian tomatoes. New Orleans culinary culture is special because our culture is blended from cultures across the globe, including Italy. When you blend these San Marzano tomatoes with all the herbs and spices, your tomato soup will be the soup du jour of your very own kitchen.

In a large stockpot, heat the oil over medium-high heat, then add the onions and cook for 5 minutes, until soft. Add the garlic and cook for one more minute. Stir in the tomatoes and chicken stock and bring to a boil. Reduce the heat to a simmer, then stir in the thyme, oregano, bay leaf, sugar, salt, and peppers and let simmer for 15 minutes.

Remove pot from the heat. Discard the bay leaf and purée the soup. Return the soup to the pot, add the heavy cream, and cook over moderately low heat until warmed through. Remove the pot from the heat and add the basil. Taste for seasoning and adjust, if necessary.

SERVES 6

2 tablespoons olive oil

1 cup chopped onion

1 tablespoon minced garlic

8 cups San Marzano tomatoes, crushed

2 cups chicken stock

1 teaspoon chopped thyme

1 teaspoon dried oregano

1 bay leaf

1 tablespoon sugar

2 teaspoons sea salt

1 teaspoon black pepper

½ teaspoon cayenne pepper

1 cup heavy cream

¼ cup basil chiffonade

Lafayette ★

SERVES 20

1 (4- to 5-pound) duckling

2 cups dark roux

2 onions, chopped

4 celery ribs, chopped

2 bell peppers, chopped

2 tablespoons chopped garlic

2 tablespoons Creole seasoning salt

1 teaspoon white pepper

1 tablespoon Tabasco sauce

1 pound Andouille sausage

¼ cup chopped green onions

¼ cup chopped parsley

Steamed Louisiana popcorn white rice, for serving

SMOKED DUCK AND ANDOUILLE GUMBO
CHARLEY G'S
CAROLE "POPS" BOUDREAUX, CHEF

Charley G's is a Lafayette favorite, known for grilling aged beef and fresh Louisiana seafood over southern hardwoods. The late Creole Chef, Carole "Pops" Boudreaux, created this gumbo recipe, helping to solidify his reputation as "The Gumbo Guy." There is no doubt that his palate and cooking skills helped to develop modern Creole cuisine in Acadiana. This gumbo, with its dark and velvety roux, has made it a staple at Charley G's for more than 30 years.

Smoke the whole duck over southern hardwoods. Reserve the duck meat for the soup and save the bones for making the stock. (Discard the skin unless you want to save it for cracklins to add to a salad or a cornbread mix. If you'd like, you can smoke the duck the night before making the gumbo.)

Cover the duck bones with water in a 2-gallon stockpot and simmer for two hours. Strain out the bones, reserving the stock.

Bring the stock to a boil. Add the roux, whisking until it dissolves, then simmer for 15 minutes. Add the onions, celery, bell peppers, garlic, Creole seasoning, white pepper, and Tabasco sauce and simmer for 1 hour more.

While simmering, cut the duck meat and Andouille into cubes and set aside.

Adjust seasoning if needed, add the duck meat, Andouille, green onions, and parsley and simmer for 15 minutes more. Serve with steamed Louisiana popcorn white rice.

BEEF VEGETABLE SOUP
MAGIC SEASONING BLENDS
PAUL PRUDHOMME, CHEF

New Orleans

Chef Paul always said, "Nothing fixes whatever's wrong like a big steaming pot of homemade soup!," and growing up on a farm, Chef Paul had a lot of vegetable soup, thanks to the abundance of fresh produce. If you want to serve your soup the way we do in Louisiana, place a heaping tablespoon of cooked rice in the bowl first.

Combine the beef stock, meats, and bones in a 6-quart pot. Bring to a boil over high heat, then reduce heat and simmer, covered, stirring occasionally, for 45 minutes.

Return the heat to high and stir in the onions, tomatoes, celery, carrots, tomato sauce, bell peppers, and Magic Seasoning Blend. When the soup comes just to a boil again, reduce the heat and simmer, uncovered, stirring occasionally, for 30 minutes more.

Stir in the turnips, potatoes, cabbage, macaroni, beans, and peas. When the soup comes to a boil again, reduce the heat and simmer, stirring occasionally, until the vegetables are tender but still firm, about 30 minutes. Skim any fat from the surface as it appears. Stir in the green onion tops and cook for 5 minutes more. Remove from the heat and skim off any visible fat before serving.

SERVES 6

2 quarts beef stock

2 pounds bone-in beef soup meat, 1-inch thick, cut into 4 to 6 pieces

1 pound bone-in chuck roast, cut into 1-inch cubes

1 cup chopped onions

1 cup peeled and chopped tomatoes

½ cup chopped celery

½ cup medium-diced carrots

½ cup canned tomato sauce

¼ cup chopped green bell peppers

2 tablespoons Chef Paul Prudhomme's Meat Magic®

¾ pound medium-diced turnips

1 cup medium-diced peeled potatoes

1 cup chopped cabbage

½ cup uncooked twist macaroni (preferably rotini)

6 string beans, sliced into 1-inch pieces

¼ cup peas, fresh or frozen

¼ cup chopped green onion tops

SERVES 8 AS A MAIN COURSE

FOR THE VINAIGRETTE

1 tablespoon minced shallot

½ teaspoon very finely chopped fresh basil leaves

½ teaspoon very finely chopped fresh oregano leaves

½ teaspoon very finely chopped fresh flat-leaf parsley leaves

½ teaspoon very finely chopped fresh thyme leaves

¼ teaspoon minced fresh garlic

2 tablespoons top-quality red wine vinegar

½ teaspoon Dijon mustard

¾ cup blended salad oil (preferably about 80 percent olive oil and 20 percent vegetable oil)

¼ teaspoon kosher salt, plus more to taste

⅛ teaspoon freshly ground black pepper, plus more to taste

CITY PARK SALAD
RALPH'S ON THE PARK
RALPH BRENNAN RESTAURANT GROUP

The views of New Orleans' City Park and its majestic old oaks make for a relaxing setting at Ralph's on the Park. To complement this leafy panorama, the restaurant's menu contains a green salad that's appealing and rich without being heavy. Served simply with warm crusty French bread, this salad makes an excellent entrée for brunch or lunch. The versatile vinaigrette can be used with a variety of salads and other chilled savory dishes. The ideal oil to use in the vinaigrette is a blend of 80 percent olive oil and 20 percent vegetable oil. The vegetable oil tempers the dressing's flavor, letting the salad's other flavors come through. When tossing the greens, it's best to coat them with the vinaigrette without any excess pooling on the plate.

Make the vinaigrette. In a medium nonreactive mixing bowl, combine the shallot, basil, oregano, parsley, thyme, garlic, and vinegar, and whisk together with a metal whisk until blended well. Whisk in the mustard, then add the oil all at once and whisk until blended well. Season with ¼ teaspoon kosher salt and ⅛ teaspoon black pepper. Let the vinaigrette sit for one hour at room temperature, then taste and add more salt and pepper, if needed. (Use immediately or store in a sealed glass jar in the refrigerator for up to one month.)

Prepare the salad. In a heavy 10-inch skillet over medium-low heat, cook the bacon squares just until the fat is rendered and the meat is somewhat crispy, about 15 minutes (depending on the thickness of the bacon), stirring often toward the end of the cooking time. Pour off all except about 1 tablespoon of the rendered fat from the skillet. (If your bacon didn't render 1 tablespoon fat, reserve whatever was rendered.) Set the skillet aside in a warm place. (If prepared earlier in the day, heat the bacon and fat again just before using so they will melt the Roquefort into the salad.)

In a very large mixing bowl, whisk the egg yolks until smooth. Stir the reserved vinaigrette well and add all except 3 tablespoons of it to the mixing bowl, then add the reserved warm bacon and rendered fat. Set aside the 3 tablespoons vinaigrette. Add the Roquefort and whisk until it is almost dissolved. Add the apples and mix lightly to coat all the apple bits.

JADE CARRADINE, *POT OF LOVE,* OTHER (DETAIL)

Add the romaine and toss with a large spoon to coat all the lettuce leaves with the vinaigrette, adding the reserved 3 tablespoons vinaigrette near the end of the mixing process, if needed. Divide the salad among eight chilled dinner plates and serve immediately. Pass a peppermill at the table.

Note:
Applewood-smoked bacon gives this salad an extra-special taste. If it is not available, substitute a good-quality bacon, preferably sliced ¼-inch thick.

FOR THE SALAD

12 ounces applewood-smoked bacon, or any good quality bacon (preferably lean and sliced ¼-inch thick), cut into ½-inch squares

4 yolks from large eggs

4 ounces Roquefort cheese, at room temperature

1⅓ cups peeled and finely chopped Granny Smith, or other green apples

6½ quarts unpacked, torn romaine lettuce leaves from hearts of romaine (from about 1½ pounds of trimmed leaves), rinsed and spun dry

Freshly ground black pepper, for serving

New Orleans ★

SERVES 4 AS AN APPETIZER
OR FOR LUNCH

FOR THE DRESSING

1 jalapeño, finely chopped

Zest and juice of one lime

1 tablespoon white
wine vinegar

3 tablespoons mayonnaise

12 mint leaves, finely
chopped

½ teaspoon salt

½ teaspoon seedless
chili flakes (or crushed
red pepper flakes)

A generous pinch of
cayenne pepper

FOR THE SALAD

1 pound jumbo lump
crabmeat, well picked

2 large ripe tomatoes

Sea salt

SUMMER CRABMEAT AND TOMATO SALAD
LINK RESTAURANT GROUP
DONALD LINK, CHEF/OWNER

As much as Chef Donald Link loves warm, bubbling crabmeat dishes, he still favors crab, cold and dressed, especially when it's super fresh and in luxuriously large pieces. The acidity of ripe tomatoes combines nicely with the crab's clean seafood flavor and a rich, creamy dressing. Peppery watercress, simply dressed with oil and vinegar, makes a great addition on the side, and creates a well-rounded salad for a lunch or first course.

Make the dressing. Combine the jalapeño, lime zest and juice, and vinegar in the bowl of a food processor and purée until smooth. Transfer purée to a medium bowl and fold in the mayonnaise, mint, salt, chili flakes, and cayenne pepper.

Make the salad. Gently pick over the crabmeat to ensure there are no shells (be careful not to shred the large chunks of meat). Add the crab to the dressing and gently fold together. Slice the tomatoes ½-inch thick. Divide the tomatoes among four salad plates and season with the sea salt. Top the tomatoes with equal portions of the crab salad and serve immediately.

ELIZA HINRICHS, *FEEDING THE HEART,* MIXED MEDIA

CHAPTER THREE
MEAT AND POULTRY

Mansfield

3 tablespoons bacon grease, or oil

2 pounds deer (backstrap, roast, or similar), cubed small (like stew meat)

Benwood's Surely Southern Seasoning, or Cajun seasoning of your choice

2 cups chopped green onions (tops and all), plus more for garnish

1 small yellow onion, chopped

¾ cup celery, chopped

2 teaspoons minced garlic

2 cans Rotel Diced Tomatoes & Green Chilies

1 (15 to 16-ounce) can tomato sauce

Warm rice, for serving

DEER SAUCE PIQUANT
BENWOOD'S SURELY SOUTHERN
HUNTER LEE, CHEF

Chef Hunter Lee was raised a true Louisiana boy. Hunting and fishing filled his morning hours, while family-style cooking and eating filled the nights. Growing up in the piney woods of North-west Louisiana is quite different from the I-10 bayou corridor, yet the flavors of the cuisine are just as rich as the stories that surround them. Hunter's father, Benny, nicknamed "Benwood," was a tried and true outdoorsman, and his mother followed right along. The family ate everything they killed, trapped, or caught, so cooking skills and creative seasonings made all the difference. Benwood's Seasoning was Benny's original creation. Over the years, Chef Hunter Lee has revamped his father's special seasoning blend, adding his own personal flair for Louisiana cooking to cre-ate the Benwood's Surely Southern Seasoning brand of products. His Benwood's Deer Sauce Piquant recipe is one of his favorites. It pays tribute to his father Benny and brings back priceless memo-ries of that first kill of the season and the family celebration that ultimately followed.

Heat the bacon grease in a large heavy skillet or pot, then brown the deer while coating generously with Benwood's Surely Southern Seasoning. Add the green and yellow onions, celery, and garlic and sauté with the meat for about 5 minutes. Drain, if necessary. Add the tomatoes, tomato sauce, and about 1½ quarts of water. Cook down on the stovetop until the deer is tender, about 2½ hours.

Season with more Benwood's Surely Southern Seasoning until you find your desired heat. Serve over warm rice and garnish with green onions.

ALLIGATOR GRILLADES AND GRITS

SOLOU

PETER SCLAFANI, CHEF

Baton Rouge ★

Grillades and grits is a simple, hearty meal typically made with steak and served for breakfast. The meat is slowly cooked until fork-tender in a tomato-based gravy and served over grits. At SoLou, a new concept restaurant from Chef Peter Sclafani and his partners, Michael Boudreaux and Kiva Guidroz, the traditional red meat has been replaced with Louisiana alligator. The tail meat from an alligator is tender and mild in flavor, a great complement to the blank canvas of grits. Serve it for breakfast, lunch, or dinner!

Season the alligator on both sides with sea salt, pepper, and Creole seasoning. Season the flour with the same seasonings. In a large heavy stockpot, heat 2 tablespoons butter and the olive oil over medium high heat. When hot, dust the alligator in the flour, shaking off the excess, and sauté until golden brown on both sides, about 2 minutes per side. Remove the alligator from the pan and set aside.

In the same pan, add the onions and cook for 2 minutes, scraping up any bits stuck to the bottom of the pan. Add the celery and red bell pepper and cook 2 more minutes. Stir in the garlic, mushrooms, tomatoes, and tomato paste and cook an additional 2 minutes.

Deglaze the pan with the wine, stirring and scraping the bottom of the pan. Add the veal stock and bring to a boil. Reduce the heat to a simmer, add the alligator back into the sauce along with the thyme, and cook for 20 minutes. Turn off the heat and stir in the green onions and parsley.

Season to taste with sea salt and black pepper and slowly add the remaining 2 tablespoons butter until emulsified. To serve, place one cup of grits on each plate. Top with 2 slices of alligator and some of the sauce.

SERVES 6

24 (3-ounce) pieces of alligator tail meat, pounded

Sea salt, black pepper, and Creole seasoning, to taste

1 cup flour

4 tablespoons butter, divided

2 tablespoons olive oil

2 cups chopped onions

1 cup chopped celery

1 cup chopped red bell pepper

1 tablespoon minced garlic

1 cup sliced shiitake mushrooms

1 cup peeled, seeded, and diced tomato

2 tablespoons tomato paste

½ cup red wine

2 cups veal stock

1 tablespoon fresh thyme, chopped

¼ cup sliced green onions

2 tablespoons Italian parsley, chopped

6 cups cooked grits, for serving

Thibodaux

BOURBON STREET BABY BACK RIBS
FLANAGAN'S CREATIVE FOOD & DRINK
JOHN SEWELL, CHEF

SERVES 4 TO 6

2 racks baby back ribs (each about 1½ pounds)

½ cup kosher salt

⅓ cup brown sugar

2 tablespoons coarsely ground allspice berries (pepper mill grind)

1 teaspoon ground juniper berries (optional)

½ teaspoon cayenne pepper

½ teaspoon coarsely ground black pepper (pepper mill grind)

½ tablespoon garlic powder

½ pint (1 cup) bourbon

1 cup hickory BBQ Sauce

1 cup Steen's Pure Cane Syrup

Most people don't think of BBQ when they think of Cajun cooking, but the reality is that smoked meats are the cornerstone of some of the best Cajun dishes: That chicken and sausage gumbo wouldn't be quite as tasty without those smokey hints of andouille, and that plate of red beans and rice wouldn't quite taste the same without those smoked ham hocks. So here is a little something different from Cajun country. Serve this dish at your next barbecue or serve it at home for dinner. If you are looking for a side dish, Chef Sewell recommends his French Onion Mac and Cheese, found in the Side Dishes chapter of this book.

This recipe requires a smoker or large upright BBQ pit, 3 pounds of charcoal, 1 pound of pecan wood chips, and a roll of large aluminum foil. You'll also need a basting brush, tongs, and a long stem lighter in addition to basic kitchen equipment. Start your charcoal in the smoker or pit and soak 2 cups of wood chips in water.

Clean the membrane off the back of the ribs using a spoon to separate the membrane from the bottom of the rack. Mix all the dry ingredients to form your spice rub and generously rub the racks with the spice rub.

By this time your charcoal should be hot and ready. Form a pile of coals at least 24 inches from where you intend to place the ribs, then place your ribs, bone side down, on your grill rack. Add the soaked pecan chips to the coals and close the lid and vents. Thick clouds of smoke should be billowing out of the smoker. When the smoke dies down, add some of the remaining dry wood chips. If the coals are too hot and they catch fire, sprinkle a little water on top. Continue this process for 1 hour.

Preheat the oven to 375°F. Remove the racks from the smoker and tightly wrap them, bone side down, in two layers of foil. Place racks in the oven on a baking sheet and cook for 1 hour and 30 minutes.

ADISYN ESTES, *THE FAMILY LINK*, PENCIL/GRAPHITE

While the racks are in the oven, warm a medium skillet over medium heat with your kitchen hood vent running. Remove the skillet from heat and add the Bourbon. Return skillet to the heat and carefully light Bourbon with a long stem lighter. Burn off the alcohol for 90 seconds, then add your BBQ sauce and cane syrup. Simmer for 3 more minutes, then pour into a mixing bowl.

When the racks have cooked in the oven for 1 hour and 30 minutes, remove them from the oven, open the foil, and baste with the Bourbon BBQ sauce. Return the racks to the oven for 10 more minutes. Remove the racks from the oven and let them rest for 5 minutes. Serve and enjoy!

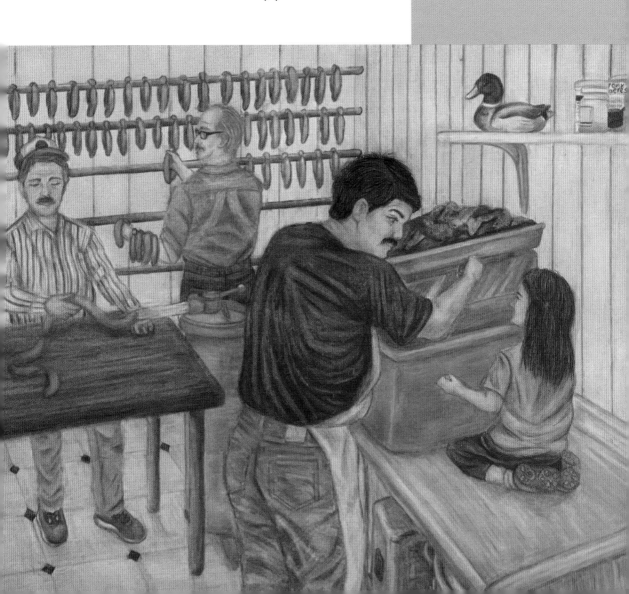

THE CITY WHERE WE LIVE TO EAT

This is the City. This is the City. The City where we live to eat. This is the City. This is the City. This is the City. This is the City. The City where we live to eat.

New Orleans is the place where the City Eats. Where the connections of food speaks to me. Feeding my soul is not a figure of speech. But it's so real to me. One day I moved out of state, and I saw that it was not the same. It wasn't until that day that I noticed New Orleans was the place for me. New Orleans has the best cuisine recipe on recipe. Fried chicken and red beans, we go to Dooky Chase to eat. It's all about Cajun food. Also known as flavor food. Brings everyone together and makes everything better. Helped the city after Katrina, a tragedy turned into something happy.

This is the City. This is the City. The City where we live to eat. Yeah. This is the City. This is the City. The City where we live to eat. This is the City. This is the City. The City where we live to eat.

New Orleans food has the power to change attitudes. It heals families. The culture of the food keeps the City at peace. There's nothing that comes close to the City we love most. We put our heart and soul into our Gumbo. It makes me emotional. Second lines on Sunday, and a tradition is Fat Tuesday. Essence Fest In the Superdome, this City is the place we call home. It's a family affair. We cherish moments that we share. We get Beignets from the Café. We eat Crawfish Etouffee and don't forget the King Cake. It's seasonal-like parades. French Quarter and Jazz Fest. We got Food and Spirits and We Dats when we come through. They scream, WHO DAT!!!

Food is the heart of the City. Say it with me. This is the, This is the. The City where we live to eat. Do you feel me? The City where we live to eat. The City where we live to eat.

JAYDA MARTIN, THE CITY WHERE WE LIVE TO EAT, SECOND PLACE WINNER - SONGWRITING CONTEST, EDNA KARR SECONDARY SCHOOL, NEW ORLEANS

MEATLOAF
PARISH RESTAURANT
CORY BAHR, CHEF, OWNER, AND FOUNDER

Monroe ★

While it sometimes isn't regarded as anything special, a good meatloaf is hard to beat! It's one of those foods that instantly takes you back to your childhood. Chef Cory's meatloaf is flavorful, filling, and delicious, and it's easy enough to put together without a lot of fuss.

Pro tips: To make this meatloaf gluten-free, substitute raw, quick oats for the panko breadcrumbs. And, for the best meatloaf sandwich ever, thinly slice and griddle any leftovers and serve on toasted bread with white BBQ sauce.

Prepare and bake the meatloaf. Preheat the oven to 350°F and lightly oil a Pyrex baking dish or large meatloaf pan. In a large bowl, gently combine all the meatloaf ingredients. (Gently fold them together to avoid making the meatloaf tough.) Lightly press your meatloaf mixture into the prepared dish, avoiding any air pockets. Bake for 30 minutes.

While the meatloaf bakes, make the glaze. In a small bowl, combine the glaze ingredients.

When the meatloaf has baked for 30 minutes, spread the glaze over the top and bake 10 minutes more. Remove the meatloaf from the oven and let rest for 30 minutes. (It's important to let your meatloaf rest before you serve it to allow the juices to redistribute and settle within the meatloaf.)

SERVES 5

FOR THE MEATLOAF

1 pound ground pork

2 pounds ground beef

1 cup buttermilk

2 teaspoons thyme

2 teaspoons salt

1 teaspoon pepper

1 tablespoon minced garlic

½ cup finely chopped celery

1 cup finely chopped onion

½ cup finely chopped bell pepper

1 cup panko breadcrumbs

4 eggs, lightly beaten

2 tablespoons hot sauce

1 tablespoon Worcestershire sauce

FOR THE GLAZE

1 cup ketchup

1 tablespoon sugar

1 tablespoon red wine vinegar

Chalmette ★

SERVES 4

FOR THE PORK TENDERLOIN

4 (6-ounce) portions of pork tenderloin

1 teaspoon lemon pepper

1 teaspoon Tony Chachere's Creole Seasoning

3 tablespoons grapeseed oil

¼ cup seedless blackberry jam

2 tablespoons hoisin sauce

1 tablespoon garlic paste

1 tablespoon ginger paste

1 tablespoon chili garlic paste

Salt and black pepper, to taste

8 whole blackberries, for garnish

BLACKBERRY GLAZED PORK TENDERLOIN WITH HANNAH WHITE SWEET POTATO MASH

PROSTART/CHALMETTE HIGH SCHOOL
ELENA HODGES, PROSTART EDUCATOR AND CHEF

This entrée won Best Entrée Award for Chalmette High School at the 2022 Raising Cane's Chicken Fingers Louisiana ProStart Invitational. Every year, ProStart students from across the state come together to put their culinary and hospitality management skills to the test. ProStart Educator and Chef, Elena Hodges, led her students to victory with this recipe for a pork tenderloin with a blackberry glaze, atop mashed white sweet potatoes. Yes, there are white sweet potatoes out there! The mildly sweet flavor of Hannah white sweet potatoes makes them great for mashing in both sweet and savory dishes.

Prepare and sear the pork. Season the pork with the lemon pepper and Tony's seasoning. In a large pan over high heat, add the grapeseed oil and sear the pork on all sides, cooking until interior reaches 145°F. Set pork aside to rest and reserve pan and any juices.

Make the sweet potatoes. Put the diced potatoes and garlic in a 2-quart pot and cover with cold water. Bring to a boil over high heat and cook for 10 to 15 minutes, or until potatoes are soft. Carefully drain potatoes, return to the pot, and mash with a potato masher. Add the salt, white pepper, garlic powder, onion powder, butter, and heavy cream and stir until well combined. Taste and adjust for seasoning.

Make the blackberry reduction. In the same pan used for the pork tenderloin, add the blackberry jam, hoisin sauce, garlic paste, ginger paste, and chili garlic paste and cook over medium-low heat until combined. Add salt and black pepper to taste and set aside.

EMMA JACKSON, *THE HOLY TRINITY,* OIL/ACRYLIC (THIRD PLACE JUNIOR)

Make the glazed pecans. In a small pan over medium-low heat, add the maple syrup and brown sugar and cook until the sugar dissolves, about three minutes. Toss in the pecans and coat them in the mixture. Remove from the pan and place on parchment paper. Sprinkle with salt and let cool.

Make the sugar snap peas. In a small pan over medium heat, melt the butter. Add the sugar snap peas and cook for about 5 minutes, or until tender. Add the garlic and salt and pepper, to taste. Taste again and adjust for seasoning.

To serve, plate the mashed white sweet potatoes in center, add one pork tenderloin to the top of the potatoes. Pour the blackberry reduction over pork, and place whole blackberries on the side, directly atop mashed potatoes. Top the tenderloin with maple glazed pecans and place buttery sugar snap peas along the side of plate. Garnish the snap peas with the pea shoots.

FOR THE HANNAH WHITE SWEET POTATO MASH

2 medium Hannah white sweet potatoes, cut into medium dice

2 cloves garlic, crushed

Salt, to taste

¼ teaspoon white pepper

¾ teaspoon garlic powder

¾ teaspoon onion powder

¼ cup (½ stick) unsalted butter

3¾ tablespoons heavy cream

FOR THE MAPLE GLAZED PECANS

3 tablespoons maple syrup

1 tablespoon brown sugar

¼ cup pecan halves

Salt, to taste

FOR THE SUGAR SNAP PEAS

1 tablespoon unsalted butter

¼ cup sugar snap peas

1 clove garlic, minced

Salt and black pepper, to taste

4 to 6 pea shoots, for garnish

New Orleans ★

SERVES 4

½ cup diced guanciale

½ teaspoon Calabrian chilies

2 cloves minced garlic

½ cup diced onion

A splash of white wine

1 (28-ounce) can peeled tomatoes

1 pound bucatini

½ cup grated Pecorino Romano cheese, divided

Salt and pepper, to taste

1 tablespoon extra virgin olive oil, for serving

BUCATINI ALL'AMATRICIANA
DOMENICA RESTAURANT
VALERIANO CHIELLA, EXECUTIVE CHEF

Domenica Restaurant, located inside the historic Roosevelt Hotel in New Orleans, is known for its fine Italian cuisine. Chef Valeriano Chiella is a native of Campania, in Southern Italy, and his heritage shines through all his dishes, including this popular appetizer. Here, cured guanciale, a cut of pork from the cheek of a pig, brings all the fat needed to render down onions and garlic and temper the heat from Calabrian chilies. The tomato-based sauce uses just a splash of white wine to bring all the flavors together.

Render the guanciale in a large skillet until crispy and golden. Add the Calabrian chilies, garlic, and onion and cook until the onions are translucent. Deglaze the pan with a splash of white wine and fold in the peeled tomatoes. Simmer gently to reduce the sauce for 20 to 30 minutes.

While the sauce is reducing, cook the bucatini in a large pot of boiling salted water until al dente. Drain the pasta, reserving a cup of the cooking water.

Add the pasta to the reduced sauce, fold in half of the Pecorino Romano, and continue to toss. If the sauce is too tight, add a splash of reserved pasta water. Season with salt and pepper, then plate. Drizzle the extra virgin olive oil on top, add the remaining Pecorino Romano, and serve immediately.

SHYKERIA SMITH, *LADY FINGERS: FROM FIELDS TO DISHES,* MIXED MEDIA (DETAIL)

New Orleans ★

SERVES 1

¼ cup Marchand de Vin Sauce (recipe follows)

FOR THE HOLLANDAISE SAUCE

4 egg yolks

2 tablespoons lemon juice

½ pound (2 sticks) butter, melted

¼ teaspoon salt

Freshly ground pepper, to taste

FOR THE EGGS HUSSARDE

2 large thin slices of ham, grilled

2 Holland Rusk toasts

2 slices of tomato, grilled

2 eggs, soft poached

A sprinkling of paprika, for garnish

EGGS HUSSARDE
BRENNAN'S
RALPH BRENNAN RESTAURANT GROUP

In the 1950's, it was customary for Owen Brennan Sr. to walk through the kitchen between service meals and ask to have his own lunch prepared. He often asked for Eggs Benedict. That's not the surprising bit. What was unusual is that before Owen left the kitchen, he would grab a spoonful of veal demi-glace and ladle it over his Hollandaise sauce. A clever chef, Paul Blangé, took notice and was inspired to create his own dish. Just as a demi-glace goes into a Marchand de vin, Paul Blangé thought Hollandaise and Marchand de Vin would make a winning combination. And, if you are wondering where the name "Hussarde" comes from, it refers to the Hussardes—brave, strong Prussian military men of the Napoleonic war, who were known to only eat red meat. "Hussarde" became known as a dish made with beef or veal stock that symbolized strength and bravery. Below is the recipe for Eggs Hussarde from Brennan's New Orleans Cookbook [1961].

Make the Marchand de Vin Sauce and keep warm, covered. (You will only need ¼ cup for this recipe.)

Meanwhile, make the Hollandaise sauce. In the top half of a double boiler over barely simmering water, beat the egg yolks and stir in the lemon juice. Cook very slowly over low heat, never allowing water in bottom of pan to come to a boil. Add the butter a little at a time, stirring constantly with a wooden spoon. Add the salt and pepper. Continue cooking slowly until thickened.

When both sauces are ready to use, assemble the Eggs Hussarde. Lay a large slice of ham across each rusk and cover with the ¼ cup Marchand de Vin Sauce. Next, cover with the tomato slices, and then the poached eggs. Top with the Hollandaise Sauce. Garnish with a sprinkling of paprika and serve.

SOPHIA BI, *THE REWARD,* WATERCOLOR (FIFTH PLACE JUNIOR)

MARCHAND DE VIN SAUCE

In a 9-inch skillet, melt the butter and lightly sauté the mushrooms, ham, shallots, onion, and garlic. When the onion is golden brown, add the flour, salt, pepper, and cayenne pepper. Brown well, about 7 to 10 minutes. Blend in the stock and wine and simmer over low heat for 35 to 45 minutes.

LaPlace

SERVES 10

3 pounds ground chuck beef

1 tablespoon olive oil, or preferred oil for sautéing

1 large onion, diced

5 green onions, chopped (reserve a handful for garnish)

3 celery stalks, chopped

1 green bell pepper, chopped

6 cloves garlic, minced

1 (15-ounce) can tomato sauce

2 tablespoons tomato paste

¼ cup sugar

¼ cup chili powder

½ cup beef broth

6 bay leaves

Salt and pepper, to taste

Oyster crackers or saltines, for serving

Sour cream, for serving

CHILI WITHOUT BEANS
PROSTART, EAST ST. JOHN HIGH SCHOOL
AVIS LIGHTFOOT, PROSTART EDUCATOR

Down in the River Parishes at East St. John High School, ProStart Educator, Avis Lightfoot, is teaching more than just food safety and knowledge. She's teaching patience, too, a key quality in today's top chefs. Sharing this chili recipe with her ProStart students is a great entryway to the "low and slow" cooking method. Everyone loves a good pot of chili, but there is always the great bean debate—to add them, or not! This recipe does not include the small and mighty protein, but it is still packed with veggies and just a bit of sugar to contrast with the meat. If you want to add beans, Lightfoot will most likely not dock your grade!

In a large pot, cook the ground beef until brown. Drain off the excess fat and set the meat aside.

Return the pot to the stove. Add the olive oil and warm over medium heat, then add the onion, green onion (save a handful for garnish), celery, and bell pepper and sauté until onions begin to become soft (not too much though, as they will continue to cook in the pot). Add the garlic, tomato sauce, tomato paste, sugar, and chili powder and reduce heat to low-medium. Cook 5 to 7 minutes.

Add in the cooked beef, beef broth, and bay leaves and simmer, stirring occasionally, for 4 hours. Take the pot off the heat, remove the bay leaves, and season with salt and pepper to taste. Spoon the chili into bowls and garnish with the reserved green onions. Serve with your favorite crackers and sour cream.

LOUISIANA CHEESESTEAK
TRILLY CHEESESTEAKS
CARLOS STICH, CHEF/OWNER

Owner of Trilly Cheesesteaks, Carlos Stich, has a love for Philadelphia cheesesteaks, so he put that love into his business. This recipe, with Cajun touches, adds in some crawfish tails and Tony Chachere's seasoning, making it the zestiest Louisiana Cheesesteak! Trilly Cheesesteaks began as a small pop-up, typically serving outside of Bud Rips Bar, before eventually moving into their first restaurant location, attached to the Banks Street Bar in Mid-City New Orleans. You can now find them just blocks away from their original location, complete with a vegan menu and huge backyard for outdoor dining.

First, partially freeze your steak for 1 to 2 hours.

Make the cheese sauce. In a small saucepan, melt the butter over a low flame. Add the flour, slightly increase the heat, and cook, stirring constantly, to achieve a medium brown roux. (The roux will take on a slightly nutty aroma.) Add a small amount of the milk and stir until the mixture is homogeneous. Repeat this process until all milk has been added. Add the cheddar, hot sauce, chili powder, and salt and pepper, to taste, and stir until the cheese is melted. Set aside.

Next, prepare your crawfish mixture. In a skillet, sauté the onions and garlic in the butter until the onions are brown, then add the cooked crawfish and continue to sauté until fully heated. Remove the skillet from the heat. Add the Parmesan cheese and Creole Seasoning and mix until combined. Keep the mixture warm, covered with foil. Set aside.

Prepare the steak. Take your steak out of the freezer and slice thinly with a mandolin or deli meat slicer. Heat your griddle over high heat, then add your steak and chop with a metal spatula until evenly cooked. Season with salt and pepper to taste.

Lastly, pour your cheese sauce over the steak (if the cheese sauce has hardened, quickly reheat it in the microwave for 15 to 25 seconds) and top it with the crawfish mixture. Put it on a hoagie roll and enjoy!

New Orleans

SERVES 3

1 pound ribeye steak

Salt and pepper, to taste

FOR THE CHEDDAR SAUCE

3 tablespoons salted butter

⅓ cup all-purpose flour

2¼ cups whole milk

2⅓ cups shredded mild cheddar cheese

1 teaspoon hot sauce (preferably Crystal)

1 teaspoon chili powder

Salt and pepper, to taste

FOR THE CRAWFISH

1 small yellow onion, diced

2 cloves garlic, minced

1 tablespoon butter

1 pound thawed, cooked, and peeled crawfish tails

1 tablespoon grated Parmesan cheese

½ tablespoon Tony Chachere's Creole Seasoning

3 hoagie rolls, for serving

Metairie ★

FOR THE TOMATO BASIL SAUCE

½ cup extra virgin olive oil

¼ cup finely chopped onion

2 teaspoons minced garlic

½ cup red wine

4 cups canned Italian plum tomatoes

4 cups juice from tomatoes

1 teaspoon salt

¼ teaspoon ground white pepper

4 sprigs fresh oregano, chopped

16 fresh basil leaves, chopped

8 sprigs Italian parsley, chopped

2 bay leaves

FOR THE MEATBALLS

1 pound ground beef

1½ tablespoons minced garlic

¼ cup chopped onions

2 tablespoons chopped fresh Italian parsley

LASAGNA REGINA
ANDREA'S RESTAURANT
ANDREA APUZZO, CHEF

When it comes to home cooking, it's hard to think of a more popular Italian dish than lasagna. Sadly, with all the frozen lasagnas available in the supermarket these days, some of us are forgetting the wonderful freshness of homemade. Chef Apuzzo named this dish after her mother, which ought to tell you something. It is her argument for always making your own lasagna.

Prepare the tomato basil sauce. Heat the olive oil in a large pan and sauté the onion and garlic until they are transparent. Add the wine and bring to a boil, then add the tomatoes, squeezing them between your fingers. Add the tomato juice, then lower the heat and simmer for about 30 minutes. Add the salt, pepper, oregano, basil, parsley, and bay leaves and simmer for 15 to 20 minutes more.

Make the meatballs. Preheat the oven to 400°F. Combine all the ingredients in a mixing bowl or food processor and mix or pulse until just combined. Shape the mixture into small meatballs, placing them as formed on a baking sheet. Bake the meatballs in the oven for about 5 minutes, until light brown.

Cook the pasta sheets in a large pot of boiling water until al dente. Remove from the water, wash with cold water, and drain.

Cook the spinach. Poach the spinach for 2 minutes in boiling water, then drain and finely chop.

CHLOE BABIN, *CAJUN CRITTER,* INK

Assemble the lasagna. Preheat the oven to 450°F. Coat the bottom of a large baking pan with the olive oil and cover with a layer of pasta, then the tomato basil sauce. Layer on about a third of the meatballs, 1 cup of the ricotta, 2 cups of the mozzarella, 1 cup of the Parmesan, and ¼ cup of the spinach. Repeat the sequence 2 more times. Top with the remaining cup of mozzarella.

Place the lasagna pan inside a larger pan half-filled with water. Set the pans in the oven and bake the lasagna for 30 minutes. Lower the heat to 350°F and bake an additional 10 minutes. Allow the lasagna to cool for 15 minutes to set before serving. Serve with the remaining tomato basil sauce spooned over the top.

1 tablespoon chopped fresh oregano

1 tablespoon chopped fresh basil

1 teaspoon salt

¼ teaspoon white pepper

¼ cup grated Parmesan cheese

¼ cup breadcrumbs

FOR THE LASAGNA

8 sheets (6- by 18-inch) pasta dough

1 pound fresh spinach, washed and stems removed

1 tablespoon extra virgin olive oil

3 cups ricotta cheese

7 cups shredded mozzarella

3 cups grated Parmesan cheese

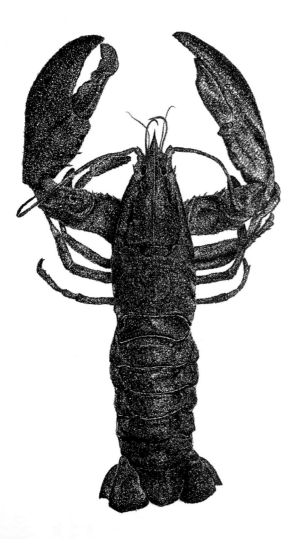

Lockport

STEW WITH A ROUX
LAFOURCHE PARISH CAREER MAGNET CENTER
BECKY LEBLANC, PROSTART TEACHER

SERVES 5 TO 6

½ cup canola oil, or vegetable oil

¾ cup all-purpose flour

1 cup chopped onions

½ cup chopped bell pepper

1 rib celery, chopped

1 clove of garlic, minced

1½ pounds boneless meat (chicken, beef, shrimp, or sausage), cut into bite-sized pieces

3 cups chicken stock or chicken broth, plus additional, if needed

Salt, to taste

Black pepper, to taste

Red pepper, to taste

Hot steamed rice, for serving

When you see the word roux, maybe the first thought that pops into your head is gumbo! However, this roux is used for a stew that's rich in taste. Becky LeBlanc, a ProStart teacher at Lafourche Parish Career Magnet Center, knew this recipe was a great way for her students to dip their toes into learning the basic techniques of making a roux. Just add in your choice of meat (see Notes below) and Stew with a Roux is hot and ready for serving.

Heat a 4-quart heavy pot, such as a Magnalite, over medium heat. Add the oil and flour, then stir constantly until the roux is dark brown. Immediately add the onions, bell pepper, celery, garlic, and meat, stirring constantly until the vegetables are soft. Add 3 cups of the stock or broth and stir until the roux is dissolved. Add the salt, black pepper, and red pepper and stir again. Reduce the heat, cover, and simmer, stirring occasionally, about 30 minutes, or until the roux tastes cooked. Add more stock or broth if the consistency is too thick. Serve over rice.

Notes:
Chicken Stew: Chicken with bones (2 ½ to 3 pounds) can be substituted for boneless chicken.

Beef Stew: Cooking time might take longer for beef to get tender.

Shrimp Stew: Cook roux to a brown color instead of dark brown. Boiled eggs can be added.

Sausage Stew: Peeled, diced potatoes can be added at the end of the cooking time. Cook until tender.

SMOTHERED CHICKEN
LINK RESTAURANT GROUP
DONALD LINK, CHEF/OWNER

New Orleans

This dish is Southern home cooking at its best—simple, inexpensive ingredients transformed into a deeply satisfying meal. For Chef Donald Link, this particular preparation is a confluence of the Southern and Cajun cooking styles that shaped his childhood; the simple, slow-simmered assembly of ingredients suggests the Southern Alabama country cooking that his Grandad favored, while the rich gravy, thickened with a roux, is something his Granny from Louisiana would have made. It's also remarkable that this Southern country dish has similarities to a chicken fricassee from France. Throw in a few potatoes, pearl onions, and carrots and serve it in a pretty little Le Creuset crock and it becomes a classic bistro dish.

Combine the salt, pepper, and cayenne pepper in a small bowl, then sprinkle the seasoning over the chicken pieces.

Heat the vegetable oil in a Dutch oven (preferably cast iron) over medium-high heat. Dredge the chicken in the flour, shaking off the excess and saving any remaining flour. When the oil is hot and slightly smoking, fry the chicken in batches (don't overcrowd the pan) for 5 minutes, or until golden. Using tongs, transfer the fried chicken to a plate lined with paper towels. Set aside.

When all the chicken is fried, add the remaining flour to the drippings in the pot and cook 4 to 5 minutes over low to medium heat to make a medium-brown colored roux. Add the onion, jalapeño, garlic, bay leaves, dried thyme, and hot sauce and cook 3 minutes more. Add the chicken stock and bring to a simmer, stirring carefully. Return chicken to this mixture and simmer, covered, very slowly for 1 to 1½ hours, or until the chicken is fork tender. Taste the sauce and add more salt or pepper, as desired. Serve the chicken and a spoonful of the sauce over hot steamed rice.

SERVES 4 TO 6

1½ teaspoons salt

½ teaspoon black pepper

¼ teaspoon cayenne pepper

1 (3½-4 pound) chicken, cut into 8 pieces (bone-in)

¼ cup vegetable oil

¼ cup all-purpose flour

1 medium onion, sliced

1 jalapeno, stemmed, seeded, and cut into small dice

2 cloves of garlic, minced

2 bay leaves

1 teaspoon dried thyme

2 teaspoons hot sauce

4 cups chicken stock

Hot steamed rice, for serving

New Iberia ★

SERVES 6

1 (3½-pound) whole chicken, cut up

A few ribs of celery, wedges of fresh onion, several fresh carrot pieces, and 1 teaspoon salt, for seasoning water

Store-bought chicken stock to supplement your homemade broth, if necessary

½ cup (1 stick) butter

1 cup chopped onion

1 cup chopped celery

1 cup chopped bell pepper

4 cloves garlic, chopped fine

½ cup all-purpose flour

2 cups whole milk

1 (10½ ounce) can cream of chicken soup

Salt, black pepper and/or Creole seasoning, to taste

1 (1-pound) bag frozen mixed vegetables, cooked

OLD FASHIONED CHICKEN POT PIE
VICTOR'S CAFETERIA
VICTOR AND CATHERINE C. HUCKABY, OWNERS

Victor's Cafeteria, located in the historic district of downtown New Iberia, at 109 West Main, has been serving up remarkably good food for the locals and surrounding communities for some 53 years. (New Iberia is the birthplace of George Rodrigue.) This dish (along with Mommie Cat's Savory Cornmeal Biscuits, page 132) was developed by owners Victor and Catherine Huckaby to serve at their charming restaurant. In fact, the pot pie appeared on the cover of the November-December 2020 issue of Louisiana Life magazine as a celebration of comfort food. Victor and Catherine invite you to come by, share a meal, and stay a while.

Put the chicken pieces in a large Dutch oven with enough water to cover by 2 inches. Season the water with a few ribs of celery, wedges of fresh onion, several fresh carrot pieces, and 1 teaspoon salt. (This will give your broth more flavor.) Bring to a rolling boil and gently cook the chicken until a meat thermometer inserted into the thickest piece is very tender and registers 165°F.

Turn off the heat. Using a slotted spoon, remove chicken pieces from the broth and place on a platter. When cool enough to handle, remove the skin and debone. When broth has cooled enough to pour, strain and reserve, throwing away the seasoning vegetables. If you have less than 2 cups of broth, add enough store-bought chicken stock to make 2 cups. Chop or tear your skinned and deboned chicken into bite-sized pieces. Set aside.

Wipe your Dutch oven clean, then melt the butter over medium heat. Add the chopped onion, celery, and bell pepper and cook, stirring, until the onion is just translucent. Add the garlic and stir for approximately two minutes, until fragrant. Add the flour all at once, stirring constantly until the mixture is a light golden brown—you have now made a roux! Gradually add the reserved 2 cups chicken broth, continuing to stir until incorporated. Stir in the milk and cream of chicken soup until combined. Taste, then add salt, pepper, and/or Creole seasoning to taste. Let simmer for 5 minutes.

Add the reserved chicken pieces and the mixed vegetables, ½ cup of the onion tops, and ½ cup of the parsley. Combine well. If the mixture is too thick you may add more chicken stock, a little at a time. Simmer on low heat for 15 minutes to allow the flavors to meld together, stirring occasionally to prevent any sticking to the bottom of the pot. Spoon pot pie into bowls, garnish with the remaining onion tops and parsley, and serve with Mommie Cat's Savory Cornmeal Biscuits.

½ cup chopped onion tops, plus ¼ cup for garnish (scallions may be used)

½ cup chopped flat-leaf parsley, plus ¼ cup for garnish

Mommie Cat's Savory Cornmeal Biscuits, for serving (page 132)

LUKE CRAIN, *ROOTS POURING INTO LOUISIANA*, DIGITAL MEDIA

Ville Platte ★

1 whole chicken, cut up (skin removed, if desired)

1 tablespoon, plus 2 teaspoons Slap Ya Mama Original Blend Cajun Seasoning, divided

1 tablespoon Slap Ya Mama Cajun Pepper Sauce

2 tablespoons olive oil

1 sweet onion, chopped (about 1½ cups)

1 green bell pepper, chopped (about 1 cup)

4 cloves garlic, minced

1 (8-ounce) can tomato sauce

⅓ cup beef broth

⅓ cup heavy whipping cream

¼ cup diced mushrooms

¼ cup chopped green onions

¼ cup chopped fresh parsley

Hot cooked rice, to serve

CHICKEN SAUCE PIQUANTE
SLAP YA MAMA
WALKER & SONS, OWNER

Chicken Sauce Piquante is a traditional Cajun recipe that has been around for generations. With a reddish spicy gravy, it has incredible flavor and is fairly simple to prepare. Served over rice, the dish was, and still is, a staple in many households in and around the Acadian area.

Season the chicken with 2 teaspoons Slap Ya Mama Original Blend Cajun Seasoning and 1 tablespoon Slap Ya Mama Cajun Pepper Sauce.

In a 4-quart stockpot, heat the oil over medium-high heat. Add the chicken and cook until browned on all sides. (Don't be afraid if the chicken sticks to the bottom of the pan or if it burns a little. This will add flavor to the gravy.) Remove the chicken from the pot and set aside.

Add the onion, bell pepper, garlic, and just enough water to cover the bottom of the pot (about 1 cup) and sauté until the vegetables are softened. Add the tomato sauce and sauté for 10 minutes. Add the broth, cream, mushrooms, and remaining 1 tablespoon of Slap Ya Mama Original Blend Cajun Seasoning and sauté for 5 minutes.

Reduce the heat to medium and return the chicken to the pot. Fill the pot with just enough water to cover the chicken (about 1 quart), cover, and boil, stirring occasionally, until the chicken is tender, about 1 hour.

Reduce the heat and uncover the pot. Stir in the green onions and parsley and simmer for 10 minutes. Serve over hot cooked rice.

CHICKEN PICCATA
MARCELLO'S
JORDAN CAUSEY, EXECUTIVE CHEF

Lafayette ★

Marcello's of Lafayette, known for using only the freshest ingredients, has become a Louisiana staple for authentic Italian cuisine. This chicken piccata from Chef Jordan Causey showcases his culinary skills by bringing together the fresh flavors of white wine and capers.

Begin by butterflying each chicken breast lengthwise, then lightly pounding with a meat tenderizer. Season 4 cups of the flour with salt and pepper and dredge the chicken breasts in the flour, making sure to coat well.

Heat the canola oil in a large frying pan to 350°F. Fry the chicken, two pieces at a time, about 4 minutes on each side, to an internal temperature of 165°F.

Prepare the sauce. In a small pot, add the olive oil and garlic and cook until the garlic is lightly browned, then add the remaining 2 teaspoons flour, making sure to stir to prevent burning. Deglaze the pan with the white wine, then add the chicken broth, lemon juice, and capers and reduce by two-thirds. Once the sauce is reduced, remove the pan from the heat. Add the butter, slowly stirring to incorporate. Season with salt and pepper as needed. Serve over your favorite pasta and enjoy!

SERVES 4

4 (8-ounce) boneless, skinless chicken breasts

4 cups, plus 2 teaspoons all-purpose flour, divided

Salt and pepper, to taste

2 cups oil for frying, preferably canola

1 tablespoon olive oil

1 finely chopped garlic clove

½ cup dry white wine

⅓ cup chicken broth

⅓ cup fresh lemon juice

3 to 4 tablespoons drained capers, to taste

½ cup (1 stick) butter, at room temperature

Cooked pasta, for serving

Baton Rouge

SAUCE PIQUANTE
WALK-ON'S SPORTS BISTREAUX
MICHAEL TURNER, CHEF

Sauce piquante is a classic Cajun cooking method used mainly for meat and seafood. With a roux base, tomatoes, and the Holy Trinity of celery, onion, and bell pepper, this tender chicken dish is layered with flavor. Chef Mike Turner is Senior Vice President of Culinary and Supply Chain at Walk On's Sports Bistreaux. His career has led him to Walk On's kitchens after working for The Cheesecake Factory, and then the Louisiana family establishment, Copeland's. His take on the traditional Southern sauce piquante turns up the heat with jalapeños and Texas Pete Hot Sauce.

SERVES 5

1 tablespoon olive oil

1 pound seasoned chicken thighs

½ stick salted butter

1 cup diced onions

2 tablespoons minced garlic

2 teaspoons Creole seasoning

½ teaspoon kosher salt

2 tablespoons Worcestershire sauce

1 tablespoon Texas Pete hot sauce

2 teaspoons brown sugar

¼ cup diced celery

½ cup diced bell pepper or poblano pepper

2 tablespoons diced and seeded jalapeño or serrano pepper

⅓ cup chopped green onions

2 tablespoons tomato paste

1½ cups tomato sauce or crushed tomatoes

¾ cup diced tomatoes with juice

¾ cup demi-glace or reduced chicken stock

Heat a heavy-bottomed medium pan or cast-iron skillet over medium-high heat, then add the olive oil. Add the chicken thighs and sear, 4 to 6 minutes on each side, until the internal temperature reaches 165°F. Remove chicken from heat and set aside.

In a heavy 4-quart saucepan, melt the butter. Add the onions and garlic and sauté over medium-high heat, stirring occasionally, until the onions are lightly browned. Add Creole seasoning, salt, Worcestershire sauce, hot sauce, and brown sugar and cook an additional couple of minutes. Add the celery, bell peppers, hot peppers, and green onions and sauté until any liquid released by the peppers is cooked off.

Add the tomato paste and mix in, then sauté another minute. Add the tomato sauce, diced tomato, and demi-glace or stock and simmer on low heat for 20 minutes, keeping the bottom of the pot clean by scraping with a wooden spoon. Add your seared chicken thighs and cook slow for 1 hour, or until chicken is tender. Serve over rice.

MYRION DOUGLAS, *MIDNIGHT SNACK*, MIXED MEDIA

PASTALAYA
SLAP YA MAMA
WALKER & SONS, OWNER

Slap Ya Mama's Pastalaya is a unique take on the traditional Cajun Jambalaya. With smoked sausage, spicy chicken, fresh shrimp, and pasta instead of rice, this dish will most definitely become a household favorite.

Season the cubed chicken breast pieces with 1½ teaspoons of the Slap Ya Mama Original Blend Seasoning. Heat the oil in a large skillet over medium-high heat, then add the chicken and cook until all sides are browned. Add the onions and cook until they start to soften, then add the bell pepper and sausage and sauté for 5 minutes. Add the diced tomatoes, tomato sauce, chicken broth, oregano, basil, thyme, and the remaining 1½ teaspoons Slap Ya Mama Original Blend Seasoning. Bring to a light boil, then reduce the heat to medium-low, and let simmer for 20 minutes. With 4 minutes left to cook, stir in the shrimp and parsley. Serve over a bed of penne pasta and enjoy.

Ville Platte
★

SERVES 6

12 ounces chicken breast, cubed

1 tablespoon Slap Ya Mama Original Blend Seasoning, divided

2 tablespoons olive oil

½ large sweet onion, julienned

1 large green bell pepper, julienned

½ pound smoked sausage, sliced

1 (14½-ounce) can diced tomatoes

1 (8-ounce) can tomato sauce

1 cup chicken broth

½ teaspoon dried oregano

½ teaspoon dried basil

½ teaspoon dried thyme

12 ounces large (26/35) fresh shrimp, peeled and deveined

¼ cup fresh parsley, chopped

8 ounces penne pasta, cooked according to package directions, for serving

New Orleans ★

SERVES 4

FOR THE CANDIED KUMQUATS

½ cup sugar

½ cup kumquats, quartered

1 tablespoon lemon juice

FOR THE CORIANDER SPICE MIX

1½ teaspoons whole coriander seeds

½ teaspoon whole fennel seeds

¼ teaspoon whole caraway seeds

CORIANDER-CRUSTED DUCK BREAST WITH CANDIED KUMQUATS AND ROASTED SQUASH

NEW ORLEANS CULINARY & HOSPITALITY INSTITUTE (NOCHI)

REBECCA KLASKALA, CULINARY ARTS INSTRUCTOR

NOCHI's accelerated six-month certificate program culminates with a pop-up café conceptualized and operated by students, serving as a capstone course and something of a "final exam" shortly before graduation. This recipe takes its inspiration from Hearth, the Winter 2022 cohort's concept. It's a technical recipe, but each of the sub-recipes is quite simple and can easily be made in advance to save time before dinner. In the end, the plated dish is greater than the sum of its parts—the sweet, tart, and acidic elements offset the rich fattiness of the duck. It's a great way to capitalize on some of Louisiana's best local ingredients.

Make the candied kumquats. In a saucepan, combine the sugar and ¼ cup water over low heat, stirring regularly until all sugar is dissolved. Add the kumquats to the syrup. Increase the heat to medium and bring to a simmer, stirring occasionally, until the kumquats are syrupy. (They will become stickier as they cool.) Remove pan from the heat and add the lemon juice. Set aside. (Once cooled, the candied kumquats can be stored in the refrigerator for up to 3 months.)

Make the coriander spice mix. In a skillet, combine the seeds and toast over medium heat for about two minutes, or until aromatic, tossing often to avoid burning. Immediately transfer the seeds to a mortar and pestle or a spice grinder and crush roughly. Set aside.

Roast the squash and shallots. Preheat the oven to 375°F. In a mixing bowl, toss the squash and shallots with the oil and season with salt and pepper. Spread the vegetables in an even layer on a sheet pan and roast for 15 to 20 minutes, or until the squash and shallots are tender and the shallots are barely browned. Set aside.

Roast the duck and finish the dish. Preheat the oven to 400°F. Pat the duck breasts dry with a towel and season generously with salt and pepper on all sides. Place the duck breasts, skin side down, in a cold ovenproof skillet (preferably cast iron) and press them flat. (Don't overcrowd; work in batches or use more than one pan, if needed.) Turn the heat to low and cook slowly to render fat from the skin. (This is a low and slow process; do not rush. The goal here is to melt the fat. The duck meat itself should remain rare at this time.)

When about three-fourths of the fat has melted from the duck skin, pour off all but 2 tablespoons of the duck fat (reserve the excess fat for future use). Turn up the heat to medium-high and continue to cook the duck until the color of the skin is caramel brown. Take the duck breasts out of the pan and brush the skin with honey.

Return the breasts to the skillet, skin side up, and transfer to the oven. Roast until the duck is mid-rare (approximately 115°F), 5 minutes or so, or longer if desired. Remove skillet from the oven and sprinkle the coriander spice mix over the skin. Return to the oven and roast for 2 minutes more.

Transfer the duck breasts to a cutting board, skin side up. Let rest for 5 minutes, then slice against the grain into ¼-inch slices. Serve with the roasted squash and shallots, and the candied kumquats.

FOR THE ROASTED SQUASH AND SHALLOTS

Half of a delicata or acorn squash, seeds removed, and sliced ¼-inch thick

2 shallots, peeled and cut into ½-inch slices

1½ teaspoons neutral oil, such as vegetable or grapeseed

Kosher salt and freshly ground black pepper, to taste

FOR THE DUCK BREAST

4 (6- to 8-ounce) duck breasts, skin-on

Salt and pepper, for seasoning

Honey, as needed

CHAPTER FOUR

FISH AND SEAFOOD

New Orleans ★

SERVES 6

6 (5–7 ounce) speckled trout fillets

1½ cups melted butter, divided

1 cup diced onions

½ cup diced celery

½ cup diced green bell peppers

½ cup diced red bell peppers

¼ cup minced garlic

1 pound crawfish tails, or 1 pound white or claw crabmeat

Salt and cracked black pepper, to taste

Granulated garlic, to taste

2 cups seasoned Italian breadcrumbs

Paprika, to taste

Louisiana hot sauce, to taste

1 cup fish stock

1 cup white wine

¼ cup chopped parsley, for garnish

SEAFOOD-STUFFED TURBAN OF SPECKLED TROUT
RESTAURANT R'EVOLUTION
JOHN FOLSE, CHEF

Stuffing seafood and meats with other seafood, meats, and vegetables is a technique that evolved, quite likely, because home cooks needed another way to use the bounty of our waters and woods. Stuffing trout with crawfish tails or crabmeat and Louisiana's trinity of seasoning vegetables adds a new level of Cajun flair and flavor to the finished dish. You may wish to try this recipe as a first course or entrée at your next camp dinner.

Preheat the oven to 375°F. Rinse trout fillets well, under cold running water, and pat dry with paper towels. Set aside.

In a heavy-bottomed sauté pan, heat ¾ cup melted butter over medium-high heat. Add the onions, celery, bell peppers, and minced garlic and sauté 3 to 5 minutes, or until vegetables are wilted. Add the crawfish, blend well, and continue to cook until juices are rendered from vegetables and seafood. Season to taste using the salt, pepper, and granulated garlic. Remove from heat and sprinkle in the breadcrumbs, a little at a time, until proper consistency is achieved (stuffing should not be too dry). Adjust seasonings if necessary.

Place an equal amount of stuffing on each trout fillet. Roll fillets into a turban shape and secure with toothpicks. Season fish to taste with salt, pepper, granulated garlic, paprika, and hot sauce. Place in a large baking pan with 1-inch lip, then add stock and wine. Bake 15 to 20 minutes, or until golden brown. Remove fish fillets from oven and transfer to a warm serving platter. Top with the remaining melted butter, garnish with parsley, and serve hot.

SUNDRIED TOMATO PESTO SALMON WITH ZUCCHINI NOODLES

LA PIZZERIA

RANDY DANIEL, CHEF

Lafayette ★

Chef Randy Daniel's newly opened La Pizzeria in Lafayette serves more than just pizza. The Italian-inspired restaurant offers a wide variety of pastas, too. He created this recipe with zoodles (aka zucchini noodles) as a healthy option. Adults and kids alike love the dish. Beyond being healthy, it's just darn good!

SERVES 4

4 pieces of Atlantic salmon

Savory salmon seasoning, to taste

2 tablespoons olive oil, divided

¾ cup sundried tomato pesto, divided

10 ounces zucchini noodles

¼ cup Parmesan cheese, for garnish

Season the salmon with the savory salmon seasoning. Add 1 tablespoon of the olive oil to a skillet over medium-high heat and let it heat up until it's good and hot. Place the salmon, skin side down, in the skillet and cook for 5 minutes, then reduce heat to medium. Flip the fish over, topping each piece with 1 tablespoon of sundried tomato pesto, and cook for another 2 to 4 minutes, or until it's done.

In a separate pan, heat up the remaining tablespoon of olive oil over medium-high heat until it's good and hot. Add the zucchini noodles and toss with the remaining sundried tomato pesto. Cook to desired consistency. Serve the salmon on a bed of zucchini noodles and garnish with the Parmesan cheese.

Eunice ★

MAKES 6 ROLLS

1 cup sushi rice

¼ cup rice wine vinegar

2 tablespoons soy sauce

½ teaspoon fish sauce

¼ teaspoon ginger powder

Half of a red onion

1 avocado

1 English cucumber

½ pound salmon with skin

¼ teaspoon salt

½ teaspoon freshly ground black pepper

1 tablespoon rubbed sage

1 tablespoon tarragon (fresh or dried)

Olive oil, to coat the pan

6 seaweed wraps

"AKA" SALMON SUSHI ROLL
EUNICE CAREER & TECHNICAL EDUCATION CENTER
AIMEE SUMMERLIN, PROSTART INSTRUCTOR
DYLAN FUSELIER AND BAYLIE GULLORY, PROSTART STUDENTS

The Eunice Career & Technical Education Center is a technical school offering hands-on job education in a variety of areas. Their mission is to provide students with the necessary skills in their area of interest so that they will be able to compete in today's job market. This salmon sushi roll recipe was created by ProStart students Dylan Fuselier and Baylie Gullory. Inspiration came from "Aka," (pronounced ah-kah), their favorite anime character.

Make the sushi rice. Cook the rice in a rice cooker. (Or boil the rice in 2 cups of water in a small saucepan over high heat, then cover, reduce heat to low, and steam for 20 minutes.) Once the rice is cooked, let it sit in the rice pot for about 15 minutes. Spread the rice out on a small baking sheet and season with the rice wine vinegar. Place in the refrigerator to cool.

While the rice cools, make the sauce. Mix the soy sauce, fish sauce, and ginger powder in a small bowl. Place in the refrigerator to chill.

Prepare the vegetables. Cut the red onion into thin slices. Cut the avocado into julienne-size pieces. Cut the cucumber into julienne-size pieces. Set aside.

Cook the salmon. Season the salmon with the salt, pepper, rubbed sage, and tarragon. Coat the bottom of a sauté pan with the olive oil and heat the pan over medium high until hot but not smoking. Place the salmon in the pan, skin side down, and cook for about 5 minutes, then turn the fish over with a spatula and cook for about five minutes more. Transfer salmon to a bowl, then remove skin and shred salmon.

Form the sushi rolls. Remove rice from the fridge. Prepare your work area with all ingredients (chilled rice, shredded salmon, red onion slices, cucumber slices, avocado julienne, 6 seaweed wraps) on hand and your rolling mat in easy reach.

Place a seaweed wrap onto the sushi roller. Wet your fingers. Spoon about 3 tablespoons of rice onto the seaweed wrap. Gently spread the rice around, getting a nice even layer, about ¼-inch thick. Layer on about one-sixth of the red onion slices, the cucumber slices, and then the avocado. Place about one-sixth of the shredded salmon along the sides of the vegetables. Tightly roll the seaweed wrap using the sushi roller. Make 5 more rolls in the same manner.

Wet a sharp knife and cut the sushi into ½-inch-thick slices. Place cut rolls on their sides and plate on a dish. Serve the rolls with the reserved sauce.

Notes:
If you would like, you could put the rice on the outside of the seaweed wraps to keep them intact.

You could also cook the salmon in red wine vinegar instead of olive oil to give it more flavor.

YUTING LIN, *CHEERS!,* OTHER

SNAPPER FOIE GRAS SASHIMI

THE SUSHI BAR CO.
RODNEY BONSACK, CHEF

Covington

Rock-n-Saké Bar & Sushi, New Orleans, expanded to the North Shore with a sister location in historic downtown Covington—The Sushi Bar Co., located at 528 N Columbia Street. In this dish, red snapper is topped with seared foie gras and finished with a honey truffle sauce.

Using a long slicing knife, thinly slice the red snapper into 5 to 8 pieces (sashimi).

Heat up a cast iron skillet until it reaches medium-low heat.

While the skillet is heating up, slice the foie gras into four pieces.

Place the foie gras in the warm skillet and sear both sides to a golden brown. Transfer to a plate and set aside.

Pour the rendered fat left in the skillet into a mixing bowl and add the honey, eel sauce, garlic olive oil, and truffle oil, whisking to combine. Add the sea salt and lemon juice and whisk again.

To plate, take the four pieces of foie gras and cut them in half. Place the slices of red snapper side-by-side on the plate and place one piece of foie gras on top of each slice of red snapper. (You may have extra foie gras, depending on the number of red snapper slices that you have.) Whisk the sauce one more time and pour on top of the foie gras. Add a bit of the scallions on top of each piece. Enjoy!

SERVES 1

4 ounces red snapper

1 ounce foie gras

2 tablespoons honey

2 tablespoons eel sauce (sugar soy sauce reduction)

1 tablespoon garlic olive oil

1 tablespoon truffle oil

¼ teaspoon sea salt

Juice of half a lemon

¼ tablespoon minced scallions, for topping

CHLOE BAUDOIN, *CATCH AND RELEASE (INTO THE GREASE)*, OTHER

New Orleans ★

SERVES 1

FOR THE SAUCE

2 shishito peppers, finely chopped

1 jalapeño, finely chopped

1 cup soy sauce

FOR THE AROMATIC MIXTURE

4 to 6 tablespoons extra virgin olive oil

1½ tablespoons finely minced fresh ginger

1 teaspoon minced garlic

2 tablespoons finely minced scallion

2 tablespoons cooking sake

Sea salt, to taste

FOR THE SASHIMI

4 ounces of Hamachi (yellowtail)

1 small piece of micro cilantro, finely minced, for garnish

1 teaspoon sesame seeds, for garnish

THE YELLOW DOG SASHIMI
ROCK-N-SAKÉ BAR & SUSHI
HARRISON BROWN, CHEF

The Yellow Dog highlights yellowtail sashimi with two different accompaniments: a fragrant mixture of fresh ginger, garlic, and scallion made into a type of soffritto (where vegetables and herbs flavor the oil), and a jalapeño and shishito-flavored soy sauce. A sprinkling of micro cilantro and sesame seeds finishes the dish.

Make the sauce. Place the shishito peppers, jalapeño, and soy sauce in a blender and blend on high briefly to form a textured sauce. Transfer to a small bowl, preferably with a lid.

Make the aromatic mixture. In a sauté pan bring the olive oil to medium heat. Add the ginger, garlic, and scallions and sauté until the scallions turn dark green. Carefully add the cooking sake (avoid direct flame!) and flambé. Continue to cook until the alcohol has cooked off, then season with sea salt. Transfer to a small bowl.

Make the sashimi. Using a long slicing knife, thinly slice the yellowtail into about seven pieces.

To serve, place the yellowtail in the middle of a plate and fold each piece in half. On one side, place the aromatic mixture. On the other side, place the sauce. Top each piece of yellowtail with a bit of micro cilantro and some sesame seeds. Enjoy!

TASSO SHRIMP WITH MANGO BUTTER AND SALSA
JUBANS RESTAURANT & BAR
PETER SCLAFANI, CHEF

Baton Rouge ★

Chef Peter Sclafani brings the sweet tropical mango to life, twice, in his Tasso ham-wrapped shrimp dish. The shoulder is a constantly used muscle of the hog, so the meat is rich in flavor, while the mango is used both in a salsa and the luscious butter. Cream and white wine soften the mango for smooth mixing with the butter, while dicing the mangos with purple onion and red bell pepper brings a cool and crunchy texture to the plump and juicy shrimp.

Make the salsa. Combine the mangos, red bell pepper, purple onion, and cilantro in a mixing bowl, then add the pinch of salt, lime juice, and Tabasco sauce and mix until all ingredients are coated.

Prepare and cook the shrimp. Soak 6 bamboo skewers in water for 1 hour. Take one strip of Tasso and wrap it around one shrimp. Wrap all the shrimp in same manner. Thread 4 shrimp on each of the soaked wooden skewers and season with salt and pepper. Over a hot grill, cook about 2 minutes on each side, until shrimp are thoroughly cooked.

Make the mango butter. In a small stainless-steel saucepan, over medium heat, combine the mangos, cream, and white wine and reduce by two-thirds. Slowly add the butter pieces, constantly stirring with a whisk, until all the butter has been incorporated. Remove from heat.

To serve, divide mango butter among 6 plates. Add 2 tablespoons mango salsa to center of each plate. Remove shrimp from skewers and place 4 on each plate on top of salsa. Garnish with a sprig of cilantro.

SERVES 6

FOR THE MANGO SALSA

20 mango slices, diced

1 to 2 fire roasted red bell peppers, chopped

1 small purple onion, chopped

¼ bunch cilantro, chopped

A pinch of salt

Juice of 1 lime

1 tablespoon Tabasco sauce

FOR THE SHRIMP

24 (½-inch-wide) strips of sliced Tasso ham

24 jumbo Gulf shrimp, peeled, deveined, tails left on

Salt and pepper, to taste

FOR THE MANGO BUTTER

2 mangos, peeled, seeded, and diced

¼ cup heavy cream

2 tablespoons white wine

1 pound unsalted butter, cut into small pieces

6 sprigs of cilantro, for garnish

Baton Rouge ★

FOR THE SHRIMP AND VEGETABLES

1 cup green watermelon pickles, halved

1 cup red cherry tomatoes, halved

1 cup yellow cherry tomatoes, halved

Half of a sweet onion, thinly sliced

1 green onion, finely chopped

4 (1-ounce) packages fresh basil, chopped

1 cup olive oil, plus more for shrimp marinade

⅓ cup cane vinegar, such as Steen's

1½ teaspoons salt, divided

1 teaspoon smoked ground chili pepper, divided

2 pounds colossal shrimp, peeled and deveined, heads and tails left on

2 tablespoons minced garlic

4 ounces baby arugula

Chimichurri sauce, for topping

FIERY CHAR-GRILLED SHRIMP AND GARDEN VEGETABLES
L'AUBERGE BATON ROUGE
JARED TEES, EXECUTIVE CHEF

Tees' impressive résumé includes stints at iconic New Orleans restaurants, like Besh Steak, Luke, Ole Saint at the Wyndham Hotel, and Commander's Palace. In 2004, Louisiana Cookin' named Tees "Chef to Watch," and under his direction Dickie Brennan's Bourbon House was named one of the "Best New Restaurants in America" by Esquire. Chef Jared Tees has been the Executive Chef at L'Auberge Baton Rouge since arriving in 2014. Garlic and chili pepper pack major flavor into this dish.

Preheat grill to high heat (400°F to 450°F). In a large bowl, combine the pickles, red and yellow tomatoes, sweet onion, green onion, and basil.

In a small bowl, combine 1 cup olive oil, vinegar, 1 teaspoon salt, and ½ teaspoon chili pepper, then add to vegetable mixture and toss to combine. Set aside.

In a medium bowl, combine the shrimp and a bit of olive oil to coat, then rub shrimp with the garlic, remaining ½ teaspoon salt, and remaining ½ teaspoon chili pepper. Grill shrimp until pink and firm, about 2 minutes per side. Set aside.

Divide vegetable mixture into 4 bowls and top with shrimp. Toss the arugula in the bowl that the vegetables were in to lightly coat with any remaining oil and vinegar. Divide arugula between bowls and drizzle with Chimichurri Sauce.

TIMYRA WILSON, *GODDESS OF THE SEASONS,* OTHER

CHIMICHURRI SAUCE

In a blender, add all ingredients and blend until combined. Transfer to a medium bowl, cover, and refrigerate until using.

Note:
The sauce can be made ahead and kept frozen up to 1 month.

FOR THE
CHIMICHURRI SAUCE

MAKES ABOUT 2 CUPS

1 cup fresh parsley

¼ cup chopped green onion

¼ cup fresh cilantro

¼ cup fresh rosemary

¼ cup fresh sage

¼ cup anchovies

¼ cup fresh lemon juice

8 garlic cloves

1 teaspoon salt

2 cups extra virgin olive oil

Des Allemands

SEAFOOD NANAN SERVED OVER FRIED EGGPLANT
SPAHR'S SEAFOOD
DONALD SPAHR, OWNER AND RECIPE AUTHOR

SERVES 6

½ cup (1 stick) unsalted butter

1 bunch green onions, chopped

3 bell peppers (1 each of green, red, and yellow), chopped

½ cup minced garlic

1 pound Louisiana crawfish tails, peeled and deveined

10 ounces (90/110) Louisiana shrimp, peeled and deveined

10 ounces andouille, cut into rounds

1 bunch parsley, chopped, divided

½ cup chopped basil

Cajun seasoning, to taste

2 cups brandy

1 gallon chicken stock

Paprika, for color

2 cups cornstarch

2 cups canola or vegetable oil, for deep-frying

1 eggplant

2 eggs

1 cup milk

2 cups all-purpose flour

"Nanan" is a common Cajun term of endearment for "godmother." Your Nanan and Parrain (godfather), most usually, had the family over for weekend dinner, where an array of Cajun foods was served. This seafood "Nanan" is a blend of fresh seafood and andouille over eggplant. The taste is comforting enough to bring you back in time to those pampering dinners.

Melt the butter in a large pot, add the green onions and bell peppers and sauté until soft. Add the garlic, seafood, and andouille and sauté 3 minutes more, then add the parsley (save some for garnish), basil, and Cajun seasoning. Carefully add the brandy (do not pour over an open flame) and cook off the alcohol, then add the chicken stock and cook over low heat, stirring occasionally, for 15 minutes. Add the paprika and cornstarch and continue to cook, stirring occasionally, until the sauce thickens.

While the seafood cooks, heat the oil in large frying pan over medium to high heat until it reaches 350°F. Peel and slice the eggplant into ½-inch rounds. In a shallow bowl, whisk together the eggs and milk to make an egg wash. Put the flour in another shallow bowl. When the oil is hot, dip the eggplant into the egg wash and batter with flour. Deep-fry the eggplant in batches, transferring the rounds as fried to paper towels to drain. Before serving, taste the seafood mixture and season, if necessary. To serve, plate the eggplant and pour the seafood mixture over the eggplant. Garnish with remaining parsley and enjoy!

BOURBON BBQ SHRIMP PO' BOY

DICKIE BRENNAN'S BOURBON HOUSE
DEVAN GIDDIX, CHEF

New Orleans
★

Dickie Brennan's Bourbon House is the French Quarter's premier destination for fresh Gulf seafood. The signature BBQ shrimp po' boy is ordered hand over fist seven days a week, but this recipe lets you be the executive chef in your own kitchen. Chef Devan Giddix recommends using fresh-caught shrimp, peeled and deveined, for premium results!

In a medium sauté pan, lightly sauté the garlic in 1 tablespoon butter. Add the shrimp and cook for 1 minute on each side. Increase the heat to high and add the Worcestershire sauce, hot sauce, lemon juice, cane vinegar, cane syrup, Creole seasoning, and cracked pepper. Carefully add the bourbon (do not pour over an open flame) and stir to deglaze the pan. Cook until reduced by half.

Reduce the heat to medium and add the remaining 1 cup of butter, one piece at a time, mixing until completely incorporated after each addition, and cooking until the sauce is thick enough to coat the spoon. Stir in the rosemary. Ladle the mixture into the French bread.

SERVES 2

1 teaspoon chopped garlic

1 tablespoon butter, plus 1 cup (2 sticks) chilled and chopped

1 pound small or medium Louisiana shrimp, peeled

3 tablespoons Worcestershire sauce

1 tablespoon Crystal Hot Sauce

Juice of 1 lemon

1 tablespoon cane vinegar

1 tablespoon cane syrup

2 teaspoons Creole seasoning

2 teaspoons cracked black pepper

1 teaspoon bourbon

1 bunch fresh rosemary, minced

2 small loaves French bread, hollowed out

New Orleans ★

FOR THE SWEET POTATO FILLING

2 pounds sweet potatoes, roasted and peeled

2 oranges, zested and juiced

½ cup light brown sugar

Pinch of ground cloves

1 teaspoon vanilla extract

1 teaspoon cinnamon

Pinch of salt

FOR THE BBQ SHRIMP

4 to 6 tablespoons butter, divided

1 teaspoon cracked black pepper

1 teaspoon finely chopped rosemary

16 jumbo Louisiana shrimp (about 2 pounds), peeled and deveined, heads and tails left on

BBQ SHRIMP PIE
GABRIELLE RESTAURANT
GREG SONNIER, CHEF

BBQ Shrimp Pie is considered a staple at Gabrielle Restaurant, which originally opened in 1992 on Esplanade Avenue. After it was destroyed in Hurricane Katrina, Greg and Mary Sonnier reopened their restaurant in the Treme neighborhood in 2017. Sautéed shrimp in a lemony butter sauce sits on top of a sweet potato-filled pie shell, giving this dish a modern spin on a New Orleans classic.

Make the sweet potato filling. Place all the filling ingredients in a food processor and pulse until blended. Taste for salt and sugar and season if necessary. Transfer the potato filling to a saucepan and cover. Put the pan on the stove (off the heat) to keep the filling warm until ready to serve.

Make the BBQ shrimp. Brown a small amount of butter in a skillet. Add the pepper, rosemary, and shrimp, then add the seafood seasoning and garlic and sauté over high heat until shrimp are pink. Add the stock, beer, Worcestershire sauce, and lemon juice, bring to a boil, and allow liquid to reduce by half. Finish the sauce by adding the remaining butter and allow it to emulsify into the sauce.

To serve, fill the tart shells with warm sweet potato mixture, then arrange shrimp on top and pour the sauce over and around the pies. Garnish each with a sprig of fresh rosemary.

REMY CANTRELLE, *STARTS WITH A ROUX*, OIL/ACRYLIC (DETAIL)

2 teaspoons seafood seasoning (preferably Chef Paul Prudhomme's Magic Seasoning®)

1 tablespoon finely chopped garlic

½ cup seafood stock

¼ cup beer

1 tablespoon Worcestershire sauce

Juice of two lemons

4 (4- to 4½-inch) store-bought or homemade tart shells

4 sprigs of fresh rosemary, for garnish

Istrouma ★

FRIED GRITS AND EGGPLANT WITH SHRIMP AND SMOKED SAUSAGE CREAM SAUCE

ISTROUMA HIGH PROSTART CLASS
PATRICIA COOKE, PROSTART EDUCATOR

SERVES 4

FOR THE GRIT CAKES

2 tablespoons salt

1 cup stone-ground grits

½ teaspoon each: garlic powder and onion powder

2 tablespoons salted butter

¼ cup chopped green onions

2 cups Italian breadcrumbs

1 cup all-purpose flour

1 egg

1½ cups milk

½ teaspoon black pepper

½ teaspoon cayenne pepper

3 cups cooking oil, for frying

FOR THE EGGPLANT

1 eggplant

1 tablespoon salt, divided

2 cups Italian breadcrumbs

1 cup all-purpose flour

1 egg

1½ cups milk

½ teaspoon each: black pepper and cayenne pepper

Istrouma High's vision is to provide a pathway for students to have success today and be prepared for tomorrow. The ProStart class offered to juniors and seniors sets them up for fulfilling careers in the culinary world. ProStart Educator Patricia Cooke and her students came together to create this recipe, inspired by the Cajun and Creole cuisine rooted in the Baton Rouge area. Grit cakes and healthy eggplant lay the foundation for zesty shrimp and sausage cooked down slow in a rich cream sauce.

Make the fried grit cakes. In a medium saucepan, bring 4 cups water and 2 tablespoons salt to a boil. Slowly stir in the grits, then add the garlic powder, onion powder, and butter. Cook over high heat for about 3 to 5 minutes, then reduce heat to low and simmer for 10 minutes, stirring constantly to desired consistency. Remove pan from the heat. Stir in the green onions and set aside to cool.

When the grits are cool enough to handle, use a round 2-inch biscuit cutter and shape into 8 cakes (½-inch thick). In a mixing bowl, combine the Italian breadcrumbs and the flour and mix well. In another mixing bowl, beat the egg and milk together until smooth, then add the black pepper and cayenne pepper.

Heat the oil in a large skillet over medium heat to 350°F. One at a time, dip the grit cakes in the breadcrumb mixture, then into the egg mixture, then back into the breadcrumb mixture. When all the cakes are coated, place in hot oil and cook until golden brown. Drain grit cakes on a dry, paper towel-lined plate and cover with foil to keep warm. Set aside and reserve cooking oil for frying the eggplant.

Make the fried eggplant. Cut the eggplant into ¼-inch rounds. Season with ½ teaspoon of the salt. In a mixing bowl, combine the Italian breadcrumbs and flour and mix well. In another mixing bowl, beat the egg and milk until smooth, add the remaining salt, black pepper, and cayenne pepper.

Reheat the reserved oil in a large skillet over medium heat to 350°F. One at a time, dip the eggplant rounds in the breadcrumb mixture, then into the egg mixture, then back into the breadcrumb mixture. Working in batches, place eggplant in hot oil and cook until golden brown. Drain and set aside.

Make the shrimp and sausage cream sauce. Peel and devein the shrimp, leaving the head and tails intact. In a bowl, combine all the dry spices. Season the shrimp with the spice mixture and set aside.

In a large heavy skillet, fry the bacon until crisp, but not burnt. Remove from bacon fat and drain. Add the sliced smoked sausage and ¼ cup chopped green onion to the rendered bacon fat and sauté for about 4 minutes. Add the minced garlic, sauté for 2 minutes, then add the yellow onion, celery, and bell peppers (reserving some for garnish) and cook, stirring occasionally, until slightly softened. Add the seasoned shrimp and cook on each side for about 2 minutes, until light pink. Remove shrimp from skillet and set aside.

Deglaze the skillet by adding the sherry cooking wine, stirring to release the seasoning from the bottom, and bring to a slight boil. Add the heavy whipping cream and reduce heat to a simmer. Slowly fold in the butter until melted and the sauce thickens. Crumble bacon (reserve some for garnish) and add to the cream sauce along with the shrimp. Gently flip and fold shrimp into the mixture, keeping heads intact. Remove from heat.

To serve, plate fried grit cake, top with fried eggplant, placing one shrimp on top of the eggplant and two on the side, then drizzle with smoked sausage cream sauce. Garnish with the reserved diced bell peppers, crumbled bacon, and ¼ cup chopped green onions. Enjoy!

FOR THE SHRIMP AND SAUSAGE CREAM SAUCE

1 pound large Louisiana shrimp or prawns, heads-on

1 tablespoon smoked paprika

1 teaspoon each: chili powder, onion powder, garlic powder

½ teaspoon salt

1 teaspoon dried mustard

½ teaspoon cayenne pepper

1 teaspoon dried rosemary

6 strips bacon

1 cup thinly sliced rounds of smoked sausage

¼ cup chopped green onions, plus ¼ cup for garnish

2 tablespoons minced garlic

¼ cup diced yellow onion

¼ cup diced celery

¼ cup diced green bell pepper (reserve some for garnish)

¼ cup diced red bell pepper (reserve some for garnish)

¼ cup diced yellow bell pepper (reserve some for garnish)

1 cup sherry cooking wine

1 cup heavy whipping cream

2 tablespoons salted butter

New Orleans ★

SERVES 2

12 Colossal (10/15) Gulf Shrimp, peeled and deveined, tails left on

Vegetable oil

Kosher salt, to taste

Freshly ground black pepper, to taste

3 whole corn cobs

¼ cup sour cream

2 tablespoons buttermilk

Freshly ground white pepper, to taste

Lemon juice, to taste

1 ounce of petite pea tendrils

4 asparagus spears

1 small radish

Half of a fennel bulb

½ cup fresh sweet peas

3 parsley sprigs

Sugarcane vinegar, or other sweet vinegar, such as rice wine vinegar or Champagne

GRILLED GULF SHRIMP OVER SWEET CORN COULIS WITH SPRING VEGETABLE SALAD
COMMANDER'S PALACE
MEG BICKFORD, CHEF

Commander's Palace, nestled in the middle of the tree-lined Garden District, has been a New Orleans landmark since 1893. Known for the award-winning quality of its food and convivial atmosphere, the history of this famous restaurant offers a glimpse into New Orleans' storied past and has been the go-to destination for haute Creole cuisine and whimsical Louisiana charm. The winner of seven James Beard Foundation Awards, Commander's Palace has evolved into a culinary legend. When Ella, Dottie, Dick, and John Brennan took over personal supervision of the restaurant in 1974, they began to give the splendid old landmark a new look both inside and out, including painting the outside iconic "Commander's Blue." Now under the watchful eye of co-proprietors Ti Adelaide Martin and Lally Brennan, the Brennan family's dedication to perfection has never wavered. A steady parade of renowned chefs—Emeril Lagasse, Paul Prudhomme, Jamie Shannon, Tory McPhail, and now Meg Bickford—have made Commander's Palace the world-class restaurant it is today, simply the best in the city.

Soak four bamboo skewers for 1 hour. Preheat the grill to low heat. Season the shrimp with a touch of the oil, kosher salt, and black pepper. Thread shrimp onto the skewers in a C-shape, 3 shrimp per skewer. Set shrimp aside until you are ready to grill them.

Grill the corn cobs in husks on low heat, turning every few minutes, for about 10 minutes. Remove the cobs from the grill. Turn grill to high, to preheat for shrimp. Remove husks and cut corn from cobs. Reserve corn of 1 cob for the salad. Place the sour cream, buttermilk, and warm corn from 2 cobs in a blender and purée until smooth. Season with kosher salt, white pepper, and a touch of lemon juice. Set corn cream sauce aside until you are ready to plate.

Remove any hearty stems from the pea tendrils, if necessary. Using a vegetable speed peeler, peel the asparagus lengthwise all the way through to create ribbons. Using a Japanese mandolin (or a vegetable peeler) shave the radish into thin discs, and thinly shave the fennel bulb, discarding the root. If the sweet peas are raw, blanch them in lightly salted boiling water just until slightly tender, 1 to 2 minutes. Pick the parsley leaves from the stems and discard the stems (unless you want to save them to add to your next pot of stock!). In a small mixing bowl, toss together the reserved corn, asparagus ribbons, shaved radish, fennel, sweet peas, parsley leaves, and pea tendrils.

Grill shrimp on high heat, turning skewers two or three times in order not to overcook the shrimp, 5 to 6 minutes. (High heat will give a great char-grilled favor to the shrimp with a short cooking time.) Remove shrimp from the grill when the flesh on the deveined part of the shrimp is white and no longer opaque.

Gently toss the vegetable salad with a few dashes of the vinegar and a few drops of the vegetable oil, then season with kosher salt and black pepper. (This salad does not need much, as the bright, fresh vegetables are what make it so great. To elevate the salad try substituting truffle oil for the salad oil.)

To serve, pool corn cream in the center of each plate. Place the salad slightly off center and lay 2 shrimp skewers down, using the salad to prop them up. Drizzle shrimp with residual corn coulis and enjoy!

New Orleans ★

GULF SHRIMP IN CREOLE CURRY OVER RICE GRITS
MAYPOP
MICHAEL GULOTTA, CHEF

This dish embodies everything Maypop and its sister restaurant, MOPHO, strive to achieve every day—the perfect blending of flavors from the Mekong and Mississippi deltas. Taking local foods that the people of Louisiana know and love, like shrimp and grits, and then livening them up with the addition of lemongrass, ginger, and coconut milk is a perfect example of blurring the lines between a delicious, soul-warming shrimp gravy and a bright, complex shrimp curry.

SERVES 6

FOR THE RICE GRITS

1 cup rice grits

2 tablespoons butter

½ pound shredded pepper jack cheese

2 cups coconut milk

3 cloves roasted garlic, smashed into a paste

Salt, to taste

FOR THE SHRIMP CURRY

2 tablespoons virgin coconut oil or vegetable oil

3 cloves garlic, minced

2 tablespoons minced ginger

1 shallot, minced

⅓ stalk lemongrass, minced

1 tablespoon Thai shrimp paste

1 tablespoon smoked paprika

Half of a fresh jalapeño, cut into small dice, or 1 pinch of crushed red pepper flakes

Make the rice grits. In a medium pot, bring 4 cups of water to a boil over high heat. Whisk in the rice grits and continue to stir until they begin to thicken, about 3 minutes. Cover the pot, reduce heat to low, and simmer for 20 minutes, stirring occasionally to prevent scorching, or until rice grits are tender. Remove pot from the heat and whip in the butter, cheese, coconut milk, and roasted garlic. Season with salt to taste.

While the rice grits cook, make the shrimp curry. In a nonreactive pot, heat the coconut oil over medium high heat and sauté the garlic, ginger, shallot, lemongrass, shrimp paste, smoked paprika, and jalapeño until golden brown, about 3 minutes. Add the shrimp and sauté for an additional 3 minutes. Add the tomatoes, coconut milk, and lime leaf and bring to a simmer. Remove shrimp from the pan and keep warm. Allow the curry to simmer for about five minutes more, then add the cilantro and season to taste with the fish sauce and lime juice.

LAILA MULLEN, *HOT SUNDAY AFTERNOON*, OTHER (DETAIL)

To serve, place the warm shrimp on top of the rice grits and top with the curry. Garnish with shaved shallot, shaved lunchbox peppers, and halved grape tomatoes marinated for five minutes in fish sauce and sugar.

24 jumbo Gulf shrimp

3 medium ripe tomatoes, diced

2 cups coconut milk

1 lime leaf

Half bunch of chopped cilantro or sliced basil

Fish sauce or salt, to taste

Fresh lime juice, to taste

FOR THE GARNISH

Shaved shallot

Shaved lunchbox peppers

Halved grape tomatoes marinated in fish sauce and sugar for 5 minutes

New Orleans ★

SERVES 2

FOR THE CITRUS BEURRE BLANC

1 orange, skin removed and cut in half

1 lime, skin removed and cut in half

¼ cup diced shallots

2 bay leaves

3 sprigs fresh thyme

1½ cups white wine

¼ cup rice wine vinegar

6 whole black peppercorns

¼ cup heavy cream

½ pound (2 sticks) cold unsalted butter, diced

FOR THE HASH

½ pound new potatoes

¼ cup extra virgin olive oil

Salt and pepper, to taste

1 medium onion, sliced and caramelized

2 tablespoons butter

Fresh parsley, chopped

GRILLED GULF FISH
TUJAGUE'S
GUS MARTIN, CHEF

Served on new potato and caramelized onion hash—and topped with Gulf fish, seared shrimp, and a drizzle of citrus beurre blanc—this dish, created by Chef Gus Martin at Tujague's Restaurant, is sure to impress. Chef Martin has been a career chef in the New Orleans culinary industry for over three decades. He has worked at Commander's Palace, Palace Café, and Tableau before moving to Tujague's, the second oldest restaurant in New Orleans. This grilled Gulf fish recipe is all about the presentation, so make sure to follow the notes "to assemble." After you assemble this dish, you'll give it a "Chef's kiss."

Begin to make the citrus beurre blanc. Add all ingredients except the cream and butter to a large saucepan. Place over medium heat and reduce by three-fourths.

While the sauce reduces, begin to make the new potato and caramelized onion hash. Preheat the oven to 350°F. Quarter the new potatoes and toss with the oil and salt and pepper to taste. Place on a sheet pan and roast for about 30 minutes, stirring after about 15 minutes, until golden brown.

While the potatoes roast, add the caramelized onions and butter to a saucepan and warm over medium heat until the butter melts.

Finish the beurre blanc while the potatoes are roasting. When the sauce is reduced, add the cream, and reduce for an additional two minutes. Whisk in the diced cold butter, a little bit at a time, until fully incorporated. Strain through a China cap or fine sieve into another heavy saucepan and keep warm over low heat until plating the dish.

When the potatoes are roasted, add them to the onion mixture in the saucepan. Adjust salt and pepper to your taste and sauté for another 5 to 7 minutes. Add the fresh parsley to finish and cover. Keep warm over low heat until plating the dish.

Grill the fish. Prepare your grill. Season fish on both sides with salt and pepper and lightly drizzle with olive oil. Grill over an open flame for about three minutes on each side (depending on the thickness of the filets).

Prepare the shrimp. Season the shrimp with the Creole seasoning and sauté in the olive oil over medium heat for about 5 minutes.

To serve, place the potato and onion hash in the center of each plate. Layer with the fish, and then the shrimp. Drizzle with citrus beurre blanc (or serve separately) and garnish with chopped green onions. Enjoy with a glass of white wine!

PARKER NAVARRE, *ST. JOHN'S EVE*, DIGITAL MEDIA

FOR THE FISH

2 (7-ounce) filets of Gulf fish

Salt and pepper, to taste

1 tablespoon olive oil

FOR THE SHRIMP

4 large Gulf shrimp, shelled and deveined, tails left on

1 teaspoon Creole seasoning

1 tablespoon olive oil

Chopped green onions, for garnish

New Orleans ★

SERVES 6

¼ cup (½ stick) unsalted butter

¼ cup flour

1 cup diced onions

½ cup diced celery

¼ cup diced red bell pepper

¼ cup diced green bell pepper

5 cloves garlic, minced

2 tablespoons blackening seasoning

1 teaspoon dried oregano

1 teaspoon cayenne pepper

1 tablespoon salt, plus more if needed

1 teaspoon dried thyme

1 pound crawfish tails

2½ cups seafood stock

1 tablespoon Worcestershire sauce

Cooked white rice, for serving

½ cup chopped green onions, for garnish

CRAWFISH ÉTOUFFÉE
ACME OYSTER HOUSE

In most parts of the nation, crawfish are used as fish bait, but here in Louisiana, crawfish are a delicacy. You can prepare the versatile mudbug many ways, but crawfish étouffée remains the supreme dish of Cajun-Creole culture. The smothering of fresh crawfish in a thick, buttery sauce blended with vegetables, herbs, and spices make this seafood stew truly unique to Louisiana culture and the Louisiana restaurant scene. Folklore has it that the dish originates from Breaux Bridge, the crawfish capital of the world. Acme Oyster House (once Acme Café on Royal Street) has been a go-to seafood spot for locals and tourists alike since 1906.

Start by making the roux. Place the butter in a pot and melt over medium heat. Once the butter is melted, add the flour, and stir constantly until the roux becomes light brown.

Once the roux reaches desired color, add the onions, celery, and red and green bell peppers and sauté until soft. Add the garlic and continue to cook. While vegetables are cooking, add all the dry seasonings.

When the vegetables are soft, add the crawfish tails and cook for 1 or 2 minutes, then add the seafood stock and Worcestershire sauce and simmer until étouffée has become thick. Check seasoning and adjust with salt, if needed. Serve over rice and garnish with green onions.

FAZZOLETTI PASTA WITH CRAWFISH AND CORN SAUCE
CHEF JOHN FOLSE CULINARY INSTITUTE
JANA BILLIOT, CHEF INSTRUCTOR

Thibodaux

The Chef John Folse Culinary Institute (CJFCI) at Nicholls State University in Thibodaux is the only post-secondary institution in Louisiana offering both a four-year Bachelor of Science degree and a two-year Associate of Science degree in culinary arts. Chef Jana Billiot, a Louisiana native of Johnson Bayou in Cameron Parish, is a distinguished alumna who trained in France and Chicago before returning home to serve as sous chef at the Restaurant R'evolution. Currently, she is the chief instructor of the A la Carte I program at the Institute, an experiential course involving all facets of food preparation and operations in a culinary enterprise. Here is just one of many culinary delights served at Bistro Ruth, the student run restaurant. Fazzoletti, literally translated as "silk handkerchiefs," add a velvety smooth mouthfeel to this dish, but you can substitute any type of prepackaged fresh or dry pasta.

Cook pasta according to directions on the package.

Make the corn juice. Place 1 cup of the corn kernels in a juicer or blender and purée to yield ½ cup juice.

In a sauté pan, warm the corn juice, shellfish stock, remaining ¼ cup corn kernels, and olive oil. Cook until the corn is tender. Add the crawfish tails, 1 tablespoon butter, and the Parmesan and bring to a boil, mounting in the additional 2 tablespoons butter. Allow to thicken. Season lightly with salt and freshly ground black pepper.

Add the cooked pasta and toss together to coat. Arrange in a pasta bowl and garnish with fried sage leaves and fresh orange zest. Enjoy!

SERVES 2

4 ounces dry Fazzoletti pasta, or prepackaged fresh or dry pasta of choice

1¼ cups fresh corn kernels, divided

¼ cup shellfish stock

2 tablespoons extra virgin olive oil

¼ cup fresh peeled Louisiana crawfish tails

3 tablespoons butter, divided

2 tablespoons grated Parmesan cheese

Salt and freshly ground black pepper, to taste

3 to 4 fried sage leaves, for garnish

Fresh orange zest, for garnish

New Orleans

★

SERVES 8

FOR THE PECAN CRUST

¾ cup pecans

1 cup all-purpose flour

¼ teaspoon salt

5 tablespoons cold butter

FOR THE FILLING

½ cup small-diced onion

1 tablespoon butter

4 ounces crabmeat

8 ounces cream cheese, at room temperature

⅓ cup Creole cream cheese, or sour cream

2 eggs

1 tablespoon Crystal Hot Sauce

Kosher salt and white pepper, to taste

FOR THE MEUNIÈRE SAUCE

1 lemon, peeled and quartered

½ cup Worcestershire sauce

½ cup Crystal Hot Sauce

¼ cup heavy whipping cream

CRABMEAT CHEESECAKE
PALACE CAFÉ
DICKIE BRENNAN RESTAURANT GROUP

Dickie Brennan's Palace Café has been a Canal Street staple for locals and tourists alike, since the early 1990s. Whether you're dining outside on Canal Street, or inside, the Palace Café brings your taste buds into the old world of New Orleans. This recipe for crabmeat cheesecake will melt in your mouth. Make sure to use Crystal Hot Sauce for a balance of sweet and spicy that will bring this cheesecake into a world all its own.

Prepare the pecan crust. Preheat the oven to 350°F and lightly grease a 9-inch tart pan. Finely grind the pecans in a food processor, then add the flour and salt and pulse to mix well. Transfer to a large mixing bowl and cut in the butter, working butter into flour with two knives, until dough is in crumbs the size of small peas. Add 3 tablespoons of ice water and evenly incorporate into the mixture (which should remain crumbly). Roll out the dough to ⅛-inch thickness on a lightly floured surface. Press the dough into the prepared tart pan, starting with the sides and then the bottom. Bake the crust for 20 minutes, or until golden. (The dough can be made ahead of time. If doing so, wrap dough tightly in plastic wrap and refrigerate. Allow dough to come to room temperature before rolling out.)

Prepare the filling. Preheat the oven to 300°F. In a saucepan, over moderate heat, sauté the onion in the butter until translucent. Add the crabmeat and cook just until heated through, then remove from heat. In a mixer fitted with a paddle attachment, or in a mixing bowl with a wooden spoon, blend the regular cream cheese until smooth. Add the Creole cream cheese and mix well. Add the eggs, one at a time, until blended. Gently fold in the crabmeat mixture. Stir in the Crystal Hot Sauce and season with kosher salt and white pepper. Spoon filling into the baked crust. Bake for 30 to 40 minutes, or until firm to the touch.

STEPHEN RAGAS, *THE CRUSTACEAN OF ADAM,* OIL/ACRYLIC (DETAIL)

Make the Meunière sauce. Combine the lemon, Worcestershire sauce, and Crystal Hot Sauce in a heavy saucepan and reduce over medium heat, stirring constantly with a wire whisk, until mixture becomes thick and syrupy. Whisk in the heavy whipping cream. Reduce heat to low and slowly blend in the butter pieces, one cube at a time, until each piece is completely incorporated before adding additional butter. (This process is called "mounting the butter.") Remove from heat and continue to stir. Season with kosher salt and white pepper to taste. Strain through a fine strainer into another saucepan and keep warm, covered.

Finish the topping. In another saucepan, sauté the mushrooms in 2 tablespoons butter until tender and all moisture has cooked off. (Excess water from the mushrooms may break your sauce if it isn't cooked off.) Stir the mushrooms into the meunière sauce. Melt the remaining tablespoon butter in the pan used to sauté the mushrooms and warm the crab claws over low heat. Season with kosher salt and cracked black pepper.

To serve, slice the cheesecake and top each piece with warm Meunière sauce and three crab claws.

1 pound (4 sticks) cold butter, cut into small cubes

Kosher salt and white pepper, to taste

FOR FINISHING THE TOPPING

2 cups sliced mixed wild mushrooms

3 tablespoons butter, softened

24 crab claw fingers

Kosher salt and cracked black pepper, to taste

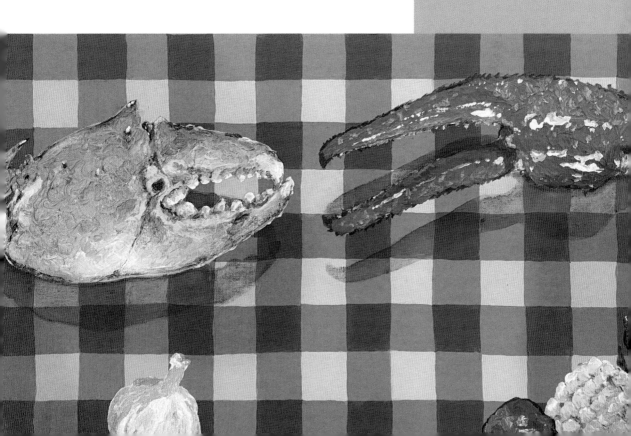

Baton Rouge ★

SERVES 6

1 pound (4 sticks) butter, cut into cubes

3 tablespoons minced garlic

2 tablespoons minced shallots

2 tablespoons chopped parsley

1 tablespoon Herbsaint Liqueur

1 lemon, juiced

1 teaspoon sea salt

½ teaspoon freshly ground black pepper

2 pounds fresh crab claws

CRAB CLAWS BORDELAISE
PORTOBELLO'S GRILL
PETER SCLAFANI, CHEF

Bordelaise sauce, a classic in Louisiana, is actually a spin-off of the original sauce from Bordeaux, France. In France, Bordelaise consists of red wine, bone marrow, shallots, butter, but here in Louisiana the sauce is lightened up with lemon juice, parsley, and Herbsaint. The buttery glaze is perfect for seafood, and, as you will see, it is a natural pairing for crab claws.

In a food processor, place the butter, garlic, shallots, parsley, Herbsaint, lemon juice, sea salt, and pepper and process until well blended.

In a sauté pan over medium heat, combine the crab claws with half of the butter blend. Heat until the butter has melted and the crab claws are warmed through. Add more butter blend as needed. Plate, serve, and enjoy!

CRAB YVONNE
GALATOIRE'S
PHILLIP L. LOPEZ, EXECUTIVE CHEF

At Galatoire's, the historic French Quarter restaurant, this topping for Gulf fish has been a hit with the lunch and dinner crowd for decades. When Executive Chef Phillip L. Lopez, a member of a world-traveled military family, arrived in 2018, he added his own global food knowledge to this recipe. The key, it seems, is browning the butter, so make sure to whisk constantly!

SERVES 4

1 pound (4 sticks)
unsalted butter

4 tablespoons fresh lemon
juice, divided

1 tablespoon
red wine vinegar

6 fresh artichokes

1 pound button
mushrooms

1 bunch of scallions,
chopped

1 pound jumbo Louisiana
lump crabmeat, cleaned

Lemon quarters, for
garnish (optional)

Make the Meunière butter. In a medium saucepan over medium heat, melt the butter, whisking constantly, for 8 to 10 minutes, until the sediment in the butter turns dark brown—almost (but not quite) to the point of burning—and the liquid is a deep golden color. Remove the pan from the heat and continue to whisk slowly, adding 1 tablespoon of the lemon juice and the vinegar to the browned butter. The sauce will froth until the acids have evaporated. When the frothing subsides, the sauce is complete; set aside.

In a large pot, submerge the artichokes in water, add the remaining 3 tablespoons lemon juice and boil for approximately 30 minutes, until the stems are tender. Peel all the exterior leaves from the artichokes. Using a spoon or your thumb, remove and discard the chokes, leaving only the bottoms. Cut into slices and set aside.

In a large skillet over medium heat, reheat the Meunière butter. Add the mushrooms, artichokes, and scallions and sauté for 5 to 7 minutes, until soft. Gently fold in the crabmeat and continue to sauté until the crabmeat is heated through. Remove from the heat and plate. Garnish with lemon quarters, if desired.

ZOE ALLEN, *A TABLETOP SPREAD,* PENCIL/GRAPHITE

New Orleans
★

SERVES 8 TO 10

1 cup Crab Pan Sauce

2 medium Yukon Gold potatoes, peeled and quartered

3 tablespoons butter, divided

3 egg yolks

About ¾ cup flour

1 dash salt, plus more for seasoning

1 dash white pepper

1 dash nutmeg

½ pound jumbo lump crabmeat

1 small black truffle, shaved

¼ cup shaved Parmesan cheese, for serving

GNOCCHI "BLACK AND BLUE"
RESTAURANT AUGUST
COREY THOMAS, CHEF

Simple and delicious. But, that said, there are a few tricks to perfectly light dumplings. According to Chef Thomas, it's very important to make these dumplings while the potatoes are still hot. The heat essentially cooks the egg yolks slightly, so you need less flour to form the dough into a ball. And having a grooved gnocchi board makes an easy job of forming the gnocchi. A simple roll of the dough ball with your thumb on the grooved board creates the desired grooved indentations on the surface.

Prepare the Crab Pan Sauce (recipe follows). Set aside.

Now, prepare and cook the gnocchi. Preheat the oven to 250°F. Place the potatoes in a small pot, cover with water, and bring to a boil. Once boiling, lower the heat to a steady simmer and cook the potatoes until soft and can be cut with a fork or spoon. Strain the potatoes. Add the potatoes back to the pot and place in the oven for an additional 5 minutes.

While the potatoes dry in the oven, bring a pot of salted water to a simmer.

Remove the oven-dried potatoes from the pot and press through a potato ricer into a mixing bowl. Add 1 tablespoon of the butter and the egg yolks and mix well. Next, fold just enough of the flour, along with dashes of salt, pepper, and nutmeg into the potato mixture until a manageable dough is formed. (More or less flour may be needed, depending on the moisture level of the potatoes.)

Separate a fist-sized ball of dough from the rest and gently roll it out on a lightly-floured surface until uniformly about an inch thick. Cut the rolled dough into 1-inch pieces and roll each piece into a ball. Working quickly, shape the dough, 1 ball at a time, with a gnocchi board (or a fork) and drop into the simmering salted water. Once the gnocchi float, allow them to cook for 30 seconds. Remove and add to the pan of reserved Crab Pan Sauce. Form and cook more gnocchi in the same manner, transferring them, once cooked, to the sauce.

Bring the cooked gnocchi and sauce to a simmer. Add the half pound of crabmeat, the 2 remaining tablespoons of butter, and the shaved truffle to the pan and warm briefly until the crab is warmed through. Serve immediately, garnishing each portion with a little shaved Parmesan cheese.

CRAB PAN SAUCE

Heat the oil in a pan over moderate heat. Add the onion, garlic, fennel, and pepper flakes and cook, stirring often, for 3 minutes. Add the remaining ingredients, then increase the heat to high and reduce the sauce by half, 10 to 12 minutes.

Remove pan from the heat. Just before cooking the gnocchi, reheat the sauce over medium heat.

FOR THE CRAB PAN SAUCE

MAKES 1 CUP

1 tablespoon extra virgin olive oil

1 small onion, diced

2 cloves garlic, minced

¼ cup minced fennel

1 teaspoon crushed red pepper flakes

Leaves from 1 sprig fresh thyme

1 sprig fresh tarragon

1 bay leaf

½ cup heavy cream

½ cup dry vermouth

1 cup crab stock

COCONUT CRUSTED SOFT SHELL CRABS WITH AVOCADO MANGO SALSA

SPAHR'S SEAFOOD
RYAN GAUDET, CHEF

Soft shell crab is a Gulf South delicacy that never goes out of style. There's something about the sight of a full crab in its shell, fried, that you can eat without a shell cracker! Chef Ryan Gaudet at Spahr's Seafood Restaurant in Des Allemands had fun creating this coconut-crusted soft shell crab. The flaky coconut pairs nicely with the light texture of panko breadcrumbs for a crunch you'll never forget. As for the sweet avocado mango salsa, a drizzle of chili oil when plating takes the dish to another level.

Make the salsa. Combine all the ingredients in a bowl. Cover with plastic wrap and refrigerate for 30 minutes.

While the salsa chills, prepare and cook the crabs. In a large Dutch oven, heat the oil to 350°F. Meanwhile, season the soft shell crabs with the salt and pepper and arrange the batter ingredients in mixing bowls, as follows: Put the flour in your first bowl, the coconut milk in the second bowl, and combine the panko with the coconut in the final bowl. Batter the crabs by dredging in flour first, then the coconut milk, then the panko/coconut mixture.

Carefully fry the soft shell crabs, 1 or 2 at a time, depending on the size of the pot, for about 2 minutes on each side, then transfer to a paper towel-lined tray or plate and keep warm, covered with foil, until all the crabs are fried. To serve, place a softshell crab in the center of each plate, top with some of the salsa, then drizzle on the chili oil.

Des Allemands

SERVES: 4

FOR THE SALSA

1 mango, peeled and diced

1 avocado, peeled and diced

Half of a purple onion, diced

1 bunch cilantro, chopped

Juice of 1 lime

1 teaspoon salt

FOR THE SOFT SHELL CRABS

1 cup canola or vegetable oil, for frying

4 Louisiana soft shell crabs, cleaned

1 teaspoon salt

1 teaspoon black pepper

2 cups all-purpose flour

4 cups coconut milk

1 cup panko breadcrumbs

4 cups shredded coconut

4 teaspoons chili oil, for plating

PAIGE SIAS, *GRANDMA'S KITCHEN, OIL/ACRYLIC*

CHAPTER FIVE
SIDE DISHES

Thibodaux ★

FRENCH ONION MAC AND CHEESE
FLANAGAN'S CREATIVE FOOD & DRINK
JOHN SEWELL, CHEF

SERVES 6 TO 8

1 pound large elbow macaroni

3 large Vidalia onions, cut in half and sliced thin

1 stick (½ cup) unsalted butter

Salt and black pepper, to taste

1 cup beef bouillon or stock

1 quart heavy cream

About ½ pound Swiss cheese, shredded

About ½ pound provolone, shredded

1 pound provolone, sliced

When you put together mac and cheese and French onion soup, you get sweet and savory flavors to delight your palate. This dish, a great new twist on those two old favorites, makes a great side to accompany smoked meats, BBQ meats, grilled meats, or you can bring it to your next potluck to make a serious first impression. Chef John Sewell of Flanagan's likes to pair it with his Bourbon Street Baby Back Ribs (see page 62). The key here is to caramelize the onions and be patient with them.

In a medium-sized pot of boiling water, cook the elbow macaroni until tender, then rinse with cool water and set aside.

Place the sliced onions in a microwave-safe bowl. Cut the butter into chunks and place on top of the onions. Cover and microwave for 3 to 5 minutes, or until the onions are soft.

Heat a medium-sized pot over medium-high heat (you can use the same one that you used to boil the pasta, after rinsing it out). Add the cooked onions and a few pinches of salt and pepper and caramelize them well, stirring often.

Once the onions are a deep caramel color throughout, deglaze the pot with the beef stock, making sure to scrape the drippings from the bottom of the pan. Reduce the stock by half, then add the heavy cream.

Add the shredded cheeses and bring to a boil, stirring often. (The shredded cheese amounts are approximate. Add enough to make a thick rich sauce.)

Add the cooked and rinsed pasta to your sauce, stirring well. Pour the mac and cheese mixture into a buttered casserole dish and spread evenly.

Turn the broiler on high heat. Top the casserole with the sliced provolone and broil until brown and bubbly. (Individual cups also can be made using this method.) Enjoy!

CANESTRI CACIO E PEPE
JOSEPHINE ESTELLE
ANDY TICER AND MICHAEL HUDMAN, CHEFS

Named after each of their daughters, Josephine Estelle reflects the collaborative spirit of James Beard Award-nominated chefs Andy Ticer and Michael Hudman. Their renowned culinary talent reflects the unlikely marriage between classic Italian recipes and the bright and mystifying flavors of the American South. With an emphasis on seasonal ingredients, homemade pastas, and recipes passed down from their Maw Maws, Josephine Estelle is open for breakfast, lunch, dinner, and happy hour.

In a large pot, bring 4 quarts of water to a boil, then season with kosher salt. Add the pasta and cook, stirring occasionally, until about 1 minute before tender. Drain, reserving 3 cups of pasta cooking water. (You don't want to pull the pasta water too early! The starches in the pasta water will ultimately stabilize the emulsification between the cheese and butter, which creates magic.)

Meanwhile, toast the black pepper in a large heavy dry skillet (the skillet must be dry!) over medium heat. Swirl pan frequently, until pepper is toasted, about 45 seconds to 1 minute. (Watch out for the sneezes!)

Add 5 tablespoons of the butter to the skillet with the pepper. It will quickly melt. Working fast to avoid burning the butter, add 2½ cups of the reserved pasta water and bring to a rapid simmer. Reduce volume by almost half (this will take a couple of minutes), then add the drained pasta.

Cook the pasta for the remaining minute, reduce heat to very low, then quickly add the remaining 5 tablespoons of butter and the cheese, stirring and tossing vigorously with tongs until cheese is melted.

Remove skillet from heat and continue tossing until the sauce is smooth, emulsified, and coats the pasta. (Add some of the remaining pasta water if the sauce seems dry.) Transfer to a large bowl, garnish with more cheese, if desired, and enjoy.

New Orleans

SERVES 4 AS A MAIN COURSE, 6 AS AN APPETIZER OR SIDE DISH

Kosher salt

1 pound dried canestri or lumache pasta (or shells, bowties, or other short pasta shapes)

3 cups pasta water, divided

1⅓ tablespoons freshly ground black pepper (not too fine!)

10 tablespoons unsalted butter, equally divided

2 cups freshly ground Grana Padano or high quality Parmesan cheese, plus additional for garnish, if desired

New Orleans ★

Salt and black pepper, to taste

1½ tablespoons vinegar

1 tablespoon olive oil

½ pound mixed mushrooms (such as chestnut shiitakes, beech, oyster)

1 tablespoon butter

1 teaspoon minced garlic

1 teaspoon minced shallots

2 tablespoons brandy

1 cup heavy cream

½ cup vegetable stock

½ cup chopped fresh herbs (such as basil, thyme, parsley, chives)

4 tablespoons grated Parmesan cheese

2 eggs

1 cup fresh fettucine pasta

1 block of Parmesan cheese

HERB-ROASTED MUSHROOM PASTA
COPPER VINE
AMY MEHRTENS, EXECUTIVE CHEF

Chef Amy Mehrtens has lived all over the globe. The Executive Chef at Copper Vine was born in Germany, has lived in Japan, California, Virginia, and Iowa, and received her Culinary Arts degree from The Culinary Institute of America in New York. Her travels eventually led her to New Orleans, where she has been able to put her worldly knowledge of flavors center stage. Once the Sous Chef at Commander's Palace, Chef Mehrtens is now creating her own dishes and delighting palates in the Central Business District of New Orleans.

Pro Tip: Parmesan is salty, so be careful with seasoning until after it is added to the sauce.

Prepare pot for the pasta. Fill a medium-sized pot with water and bring to a boil. Season water with salt. (It should taste like the sea.)

Prepare another pot for the poached eggs. Fill a small pot with water, season the same way as the pasta water, but add 1½ tablespoons vinegar to this pot. Bring to a boil.

Make the sauce. Heat a large sauté pan over medium-high heat and coat the bottom with the olive oil. Once the oil is shimmering, add the mushrooms. Do not season or move them around for a minute or two. Once the mushrooms are lightly browned, create an empty space (hole) in the middle of the sauté pan. Add the butter, let it melt, then add the garlic and shallots. Season and sauté until aromatic, about 30 seconds, then mix into the mushrooms.

Remove pan from the heat. Stand back and carefully add the brandy to deglaze the bottom of the sauté pan. (The brandy will ignite, so use caution!) Using a wooden spoon or spatula, scrape off any of the brown bits on the bottom of your sauté pan. Add the cream and vegetable stock and cook over a slow simmer until the sauce is reduced by half. Add the chopped fresh herbs and grated Parmesan. Remove pan from the heat and cover to keep warm.

Poach the eggs. The egg water should be boiling by this point. Turn the water down to medium heat. Crack the eggs into a small bowl without breaking the yolks. Next, stir the vinegar water into a whirlpool. Slowly submerge your egg bowl slightly into the vinegar water so that one egg flows out at a time. Do not stir the eggs at this point. (It will break them.) The eggs will separate on their own. Let the eggs poach approximately 2 minutes. Use a slotted spoon to scoop them out of the bowl. Transfer the eggs to a plate with a dry towel and keep them warm, close by the stove. Season with salt and pepper.

Cook the pasta. As soon as the eggs are dropped into the poaching water, drop the fresh pasta into the boiling pasta water and boil for 2 minutes. Drain and add the hot pasta to the mushroom cream sauce.

To serve, immediately take a ladle and a meat fork and swirl the pasta inside the ladle with the fork to make a nest of pasta. Transfer to a plate, then carefully place a poached egg in the middle of the nest. Ladle some extra sauce around the plate. Use a peeler to shave Parmesan from the block of cheese over the top. Plate another serving in the same way. Bon appétit!

Note:
Not ready to eat this right away? You can always make the sauce and portion it in your freezer for later meal prep. The fresh pasta will hold in your freezer for 3 months.

New Orleans

2 cups olive oil, for deep-frying

1 pound whole fresh Brussels sprouts

1 teaspoon kosher salt

1 teaspoon balsamic vinegar

½ cup toasted pecan pieces

CRISPY CRACKED BRUSSELS SPROUTS
ZEA ROTISSERIE & BAR
GREG REGGIO, CHEF

Brussels sprouts may not have been your favorite vegetable growing up, but chances are, as an adult, you've found a rendition of the cabbage-like veggie that suits your taste. Over the years, a crispy, flattened version has become popular in restaurants across the state, mostly served just as an appetizer. Speaking of how best to flatten the sprouts, Chef Greg Reggio of Zea Rotisserie & Bar says, "Don't kill 'em….just wound 'em." Flattening the Brussels sprouts is an important step in making them come out crispy. The core of the sprouts should be cracked open, and then flattened to about ¾-inch thickness. Yes, Chef!

Pour enough oil in a sauce pot so that it is 1- to 2-inches deep and heat to 375°F.

Meanwhile, trim the stem ends of the Brussels sprouts, if they are dried and discolored. Place the sprouts on a cutting board and smash with a meat mallet to flatten them to ¾-inch thickness.

Carefully place 6 to 8 flattened Brussels sprouts in the oil and fry until lightly browned, about 30 to 45 seconds. Remove from the oil and drain well on paper towels. Repeat with the remaining sprouts.

Season the warm sprouts with the salt, then drizzle with the balsamic vinegar. Sprinkle with the toasted pecan pieces and serve.

Note:
The Brussels sprouts may be sautéed in 2 tablespoons of oil instead of deep-fried, if desired.

GINGERED GREEN VEGETABLES

MAGIC SEASONING BLENDS
PAUL PRUDHOMME, CHEF

New Orleans

Chef Paul loved to combine the most ordinary ingredients to create dishes with an exotic flavor and international appeal. The combination of ginger and coconut milk takes these everyday vegetables to the next level! Chef Paul always served them with a piece of blackened fish.

Make a seasoning mix by combining Chef Paul Prudhomme's Vegetable Magic®, ginger, and coriander in a small bowl. Set aside.

Peel the potato and dice into ½-inch cubes. Remove broccoli stalks from the head of broccoli and chop stalks into ½-inch pieces. Chop florets into small pieces, reserving 2 cups. (Keep remaining florets for another use.) Heat the oil in a heavy 5-quart pot over high heat just until the oil begins to smoke, about 3 to 4 minutes. Add the onions, 1 cup of the potato cubes, the broccoli stalks, and the mustard seeds and cook, covered, stirring occasionally, for 10 minutes.

Add ½ cup of the stock, stir and scrape the bottom of the pot thoroughly, and continue to cook, covered, for 3 more minutes. Add the reserved seasoning mix and another ½ cup stock, scrape the pot bottom thoroughly again, and add the remaining ½ cup stock, the remaining potatoes, and the coconut. Continue to cook, stirring occasionally, until the potatoes are tender, about 12 minutes.

Blend in the coconut milk and add the reserved 2 cups broccoli florets and remaining ingredients. Cover and bring to a boil, then reduce the heat to low and simmer, stirring occasionally, until the vegetables are tender, but still retain their beautiful bright green color, about 9 minutes. Serve hot as a side dish.

Note:
This dish also can be chilled and served on a leaf of lettuce as an unusual appetizer or salad.

SERVES 6 TO 8

1 tablespoon plus
1 teaspoon Chef Paul
Prudhomme's Vegetable
Magic®

¾ teaspoon ground ginger

½ teaspoon ground
coriander

1 medium potato, divided

1 large head broccoli,
divided

2 tablespoons olive oil

1 cup chopped onions

1 teaspoon brown or
yellow mustard seeds

1½ cups vegetable stock,
divided

About 1½ cups freshly
grated coconut (from half
of a small coconut)

1 cup unsweetened
coconut milk

1 pound green beans, tips
removed and cut in half

2 cups chopped green bell
peppers

1 tablespoon minced
fresh garlic

1 tablespoon minced
fresh ginger

¼ cup chopped fresh
cilantro

Monroe

SERVES 4

1 pound fresh okra

FOR THE SPICY AIOLI

1 cup Duke's® Mayonnaise

3 teaspoons
pure sesame oil

1 tablespoon Sambal

1 tablespoon Sriracha
sauce

Juice of 1 lime

FRIED OKRA
PARISH RESTAURANT
CORY BAHR, CHEF, OWNER, AND FOUNDER

In the South, we are very opinionated when it comes to the foods we love—or don't love. Okra is a polarizing vegetable due to its potential for a less than appealing texture (slimy) when improperly prepared. This simple recipe circumvents the slimy in favor of crispy, crunchy goodness! Here, a versatile spicy aioli gives a quick kick to the okra. It has a two-week shelf life in the fridge, so you can make it ahead of time.

Prepare a hot grill or heat a cast iron skillet over high heat until hot. Toast the okra on the grill or in the skillet until lightly browned and crispy on all sides.

Prepare the aioli. Combine all the ingredients in a mixing bowl.

To serve, spoon the aioli onto each plate, place crispy okra on top, and enjoy the aioli for dipping. (Or you can place some aioli in a mixing bowl, add the okra, and toss to coat.)

PURPLE HULL PEAS
"US UP NORTH"
CELEBRATING NORTH LOUISIANA CUISINE
HARDETTE HARRIS, CHEF

Shreveport

Chef Harris, of "Us Up North" in Shreveport, Louisiana, loves purple hull peas almost as much as she likes a chocolate brownie with ice cream on top. Shelling the peas and enjoying a big bowl with hot water cornbread was one of her most memorable culinary experiences as a child. In fact, she says the family usually ate peas and cornbread as the main dish, instead of a side, for no reason other than they liked it a lot. That main dish could also be a bowl of purple hull peas, crowders, or speckled butter beans. Good times!

Place the ham hock and neck bone in a large stockpot and cover with water. Cook, covered, over medium heat for 1 hour, or until the meat easily comes off the bones. Remove meat from bones, saving the liquid. Strain the liquid, if necessary, to remove any small bones.

Add the peas, onion, garlic, okra, seasoned salt, garlic powder, and salt and pepper, to taste, then cover and cook for 30 minutes. Return the meat to the pot and cook until the peas are soft, but not broken apart, about 20 minutes more. Adjust seasonings. Serve with cornbread, sliced yellow onion, and sliced tomato.

Note:
This recipe represents authentic, rural southern cooking. Feel free to adjust meat and seasonings to your taste.

SERVES 6 TO 8

1 large smoked ham hock, rinsed and patted dry

1 large smoked pork neck bone, rinsed and patted dry

1 to 2 pounds fresh purple hull peas, rinsed

Half of a yellow onion, sliced

2 garlic cloves, minced

1 to 2 okra pods, whole or chopped, to thicken

1 tablespoon seasoned salt

1 teaspoon garlic powder

Salt and black pepper, to taste

Cornbread, fresh sliced yellow onion, and sliced tomato, for serving

ZOE ANDERSON, *MOM'S RED BEANS*, PENCIL/GRAPHITE

New Orleans

SERVES 6

2 tablespoons unsalted butter, melted, for brushing, plus ½ cup unsalted butter, cut into small cubes

About 8 anchovy fillets (more or less, as desired)

1 pint heavy cream

1 lemon, zested

4 to 5 large russet potatoes

Salt and freshly ground pepper

Canola or grapeseed oil, for shallow-frying

Sea salt, for finishing the dish

PAVÉ POTATOES WITH ANCHOVY
SEAWORTHY
KRISTEN YORK, CHEF

Seaworthy showcases wild-caught and sustainably-harvested oysters from American waters—Gulf Coast, East Coast, and West Coast alike—as well as locally sourced fish and game. Set in a classic Creole cottage built in 1832, Seaworthy was opened by Ace Hotel with support from the team at Grand Banks. The restaurant culls inspiration from Gulf Coast waterways, the time-worn traditions of Southern hospitality, and the legendary exuberance of the city of New Orleans.

Preheat the oven to 350°F. Cover a 13- by 9-inch baking pan or casserole dish with two sheets of parchment paper (to create neat corners), leaving a 5- or 6-inch overhang on all sides. Brush with the melted butter and set aside.

On a cutting board, using the edge of a sharp knife, scrape the anchovies into a paste. In a large bowl, whisk (briefly) the anchovy paste into the heavy cream. (Anchovies are taking the place of salt in this recipe and adding some umami to the potatoes, so add as desired.) Add the lemon zest to the anchovy-cream mixture.

Peel the potatoes and submerge in cold water. Working with one dry potato at a time, and using a mandolin, slice the potato into long, thin strips (1-millimeter thick) and transfer to the anchovy-cream mixture, tossing to make sure slices are well coated. Slice and coat the remaining potatoes in the same way.

When all the potatoes are sliced and coated with the anchovy-cream mixture, begin to layer the potatoes, one layer at a time, in the prepared baking pan. (The layers should be as even as possible, and each layer should be formed in an alternating direction.) Every three layers, add several small cubes of butter and season with salt and pepper. Repeat this until you have about 1½ inches in depth. When you complete the last layer, fold the edges of the parchment over the potatoes. Cover tightly with aluminum foil and bake for 1 hour, or until the potatoes are golden and bubbling.

KANE GRANGER, *LOUISIANA FAMILY TRADITIONS*, OTHER (DETAIL)

Remove pan from oven, uncover, and let cool completely to room temperature. When cool, cover the top with foil and press down to touch the potatoes. Use cans to weigh the potato terrine down and refrigerate overnight.

The next day, run a knife around the edge of the pavé and unmold onto a cutting board. Cut into 1-inch cubes. (The parchment will stick to the pan, so give the pan a good bang on the bottom. If the pavé is too difficult to unmold, you can cut it into cubes in the pan and scoop them out with a flexible spatula.) Heat 1-inch of the cooking oil in a skillet and shallow-fry the cubes, in batches, being sure to flip occasionally with tongs or chop sticks, until browned evenly. Sprinkle with sea salt and serve immediately.

New Iberia

MAKES 12 TO 14 BISCUITS

2 cups self-rising flour

1 teaspoon baking powder

½ cup (1 stick) cold butter (place in freezer 30 minutes before use)

1 (8.5-ounce) box Jiffy brand corn muffin mix

1 tablespoon Everything Bagel Seasoning (preferably Trader Joe's or Costco's versions)

1 egg, cold

1 cup whole-fat buttermilk (preferably Bulgarian-style, sold at Super 1 Foods), plus more if necessary

All-purpose flour, for dusting

Melted butter, for brushing tops, if desired

MOMMIE CAT'S SAVORY CORNMEAL BISCUITS
VICTOR'S CAFETERIA
VICTOR AND CATHERINE C. HUCKABY, OWNERS

These biscuits were developed to accompany Old Fashioned Chicken Pot Pie (page 78). They are called "Mommie Cat's" because the Huckaby's grandchildren were the taste testers for this recipe.

Preheat the oven to 400°F and put oven rack in middle of oven. Line a baking sheet with parchment paper. In a medium bowl, whisk together the self-rising flour and baking powder. Using the large holes of a box grater, grate the cold butter directly into the flour mixture. Using a fork, work the butter into the flour mixture until it resembles large crumbs. Add the Jiffy mix and Everything Bagel Seasoning and lightly mix in with a fork. Add the egg and buttermilk, and with the same fork, gently mix until it becomes a sticky ball of dough. (You may need to add an additional 1 to 2 tablespoons of buttermilk to make this happen.)

Place ball of dough on a well-floured work surface. Sprinkle the top lightly with flour and cover with a tea towel. Allow to rest 15 minutes. (You can use this time to clean up!)

Remove tea towel, dust dough ball with flour, and knead gently for 90 seconds. Press or roll out (gently!) to ½-inch thickness. Using a 2½-inch biscuit cutter, cut and place biscuits, sides touching, on the parchment-lined baking sheet. For better browning, brush tops with melted butter.

Bake biscuits on middle rack for approximately 15 minutes, until golden brown. Serve with the pot pie, or simply, just as the Huckaby grandchildren like them, with butter, honey, and milk.

MAMA JEN'S CAJUN CORN BREAD
SLAP YA MAMA
WALTER & SONS, OWNERS

Mama Jen Walker is one of the founders of Slap Ya Mama Louisiana Food Products. Of all her recipes, Mama Jen's Cajun cornbread is probably her most recognized. Anytime there is a family event, she makes her famous cornbread, and it isn't long before the whole tray is gone. You need to move quickly when she places her cornbread on the serving table, or you'll come up empty-handed.

Preheat the oven to 350°F. Grease a 13- by 9-inch baking pan with butter. In a medium skillet, cook the Tasso and sausage over medium-high heat, stirring frequently, until browned, 5 to 7 minutes. Set aside.

In a large bowl, stir together the cornmeal, Slap Ya Mama Original Blend Cajun Seasoning, and baking soda with a fork. Add the corn, milk, oil, and eggs, stirring until well combined. Add the reserved Tasso and sausage, cheese, onion, bell pepper, and jalapeño, stirring until well combined, and spoon into prepared pan.

Bake until a wooden pick inserted in center comes out clean and top is golden brown, about 55 minutes. Let cool for 30 minutes before serving.

Ville Platte
★

SERVES 10 TO 12

1 tablespoon unsalted butter

1 cup diced smoked Tasso or ham

1 cup diced smoked sausage

1 cup yellow cornmeal

1 tablespoon Slap Ya Mama Original Blend Cajun Seasoning

1 teaspoon baking soda

1 (14.75-ounce) can cream-style corn

1 cup whole milk

½ cup vegetable oil

2 large eggs, beaten

2½ cups shredded mild cheddar cheese

1 small onion, finely chopped (about 1 cup)

1 medium green bell pepper, seeded and diced (about 1 cup)

3 medium jalapeños, seeded and minced (about ½ cup)

SPICY-SWEET AIOLI
W. D. & MARY BAKER SMITH CAREER CENTER
KANDICE DEQUEANT, PROSTART EDUCATOR

If you are looking to add extra flavor to just about anything, aioli is a great way to do it. Typically made with an emulsion of garlic and olive oil, this mayo-based recipe adds sweet heat from Sriracha and honey. You can spread the aioli on your hot dog bun, sandwich, or burger bun. It even makes a great dip for soft pretzels. ProStart Educator Kandice Dequeant created this recipe for her students to help them gain mastery of measuring ingredients with tablespoons. Perfecting this skill, especially with sauces, assures the right viscosity every time.

Combine the mayonnaise, honey, and Sriracha sauce in a small bowl and serve immediately, or chill for later use. Stir the parsley into the aioli, or if you prefer, sprinkle the parsley over the plated aioli, to garnish.

Lafayette ★

MAKES ABOUT ¾ CUP

6 tablespoons mayonnaise

2 tablespoons honey

2 tablespoons Sriracha sauce

1 tablespoon minced parsley, for garnish

EMILY BONIN, *LES CADIEN,* MIXED MEDIA (FOURTH PLACE JUNIOR)

CHAPTER SIX
DESSERTS

New Iberia

MAKES 1 (10-INCH) PIE

3¼ cups whole milk

3 eggs

1½ cups sugar

¼ teaspoon salt

½ cup cornstarch

¼ cup (½ stick) unsalted butter, cut into pieces

1½ teaspoons vanilla extract

2 cups sweetened flaked coconut (preferably Baker's)

1 (10-inch) deep pie shell, baked and cooled

1 (12-ounce) container frozen whipped topping, thawed, for topping

¼ cup toasted coconut, for garnish

COCONUT PIE
VICTOR'S CAFETERIA
VICTOR AND CATHERINE C. HUCKABY, OWNERS

The Huckaby's have been serving Coconut Pie at their business, Victor's Cafeteria, for over 50 years, and it is their most popular dessert. In fact, this pie even made the cover of the April-May 2008 issue of Taste of the South magazine. The title was Coconut Pie—Easy! Creamy! Scrumptious! We think you'll agree on all counts!

Heat the milk in a medium-sized saucepan over low heat and bring to a slow simmer.

While the milk is heating, using an electric mixer, beat together the eggs, sugar, salt, and cornstarch, beginning on medium speed and increasing to high speed, until the mixture is thick and light in color. (It should look like pudding. Be sure to beat well.)

Once the milk in bubbling, add the egg mixture slowly, whisking constantly until thick. (It will thicken quickly.) Lower the heat and continue stirring with the whisk until the custard "breaks wind" (meaning air bubbles break on the surface), then whisk for 2 minutes more.

Remove the custard from the heat. Add the butter and vanilla, whisking until completely combined. Fold in the coconut. Pour into the cooled pie shell and cover with a film of plastic wrap to prevent a "skin" from forming on the surface. Place the pie in the refrigerator for several hours or overnight to chill and thicken.

To serve, remove plastic wrap and top with whipped topping, making swirls. Garnish top with toasted coconut. Enjoy!

CLASSIC PECAN PIE
CANE RIVER PECAN COMPANY

Get ready to impress your family and friends during the holiday season (or year-round, why not?) by whipping up a scrumptious old-fashioned dessert–Cane River's Classic Pecan Pie! Loaded with pecans, this is the perfect Southern pie recipe. It's easy enough for beginner bakers everywhere, so don't forget to get your kids involved, too.

Make the pie crust. In a large bowl, using your hands, mix the flour and butter with 2 tablespoons of cool water. Form the dough into a ball and transfer to a 9-inch pie pan or black iron skillet. Using your fingers, slowly work the dough evenly into the bottom and up the sides of the pie pan or skillet.

Make the pie filling and bake the pie. Preheat the oven to 350°F. Toast the pecan halves for 9 minutes and then set aside to cool.

While toasting the pecans, melt the butter and set aside. Beat 3 of the eggs and set them aside as well.

In a large bowl, stir together the sugar, salt, corn syrup, molasses, and vanilla extract. Fold in the beaten eggs and melted butter.

Arrange the toasted pecan halves in a circular pattern on the bottom of the pie crust. Slowly pour the pie filling mixture over the pecan halves. In a small bowl, make an egg wash by beating together the remaining egg and 1 teaspoon of cool water. Brush the egg wash onto the exposed pie crust. Using a fork, crimp the pie crust edges.

Place the pie in the oven on the bottom rack and bake for 1 hour. The pecan halves will rise to the top of the pie during baking. Remove pie and let cool for at least two hours. Enjoy!

Note:
For a boozy pecan pie, add 2 tablespoons of your preferred bourbon to the pie filling. Once the pie has cooled, brush a little more bourbon on top of the pie and pie crust. (We prefer Elijah Craig Small Batch Kentucky Straight Bourbon Whiskey.)

New Iberia ★

MAKES 1 (9-INCH) PIE

FOR THE PIE CRUST

1 cup flour

½ cup (1 stick) butter, at room temperature

FOR THE PIE FILLING

1 cup Mammoth Cane River pecan halves

½ cup (1 stick) butter

4 eggs, divided

1 cup sugar

⅛ teaspoon salt

1 cup Karo light corn syrup

1 tablespoon Steen's dark molasses

2 teaspoons vanilla extract

New Iberia ★

MAKES ENOUGH FILLING
FOR A 9-INCH, 3-LAYER CAKE

1 cup sugar

1 tablespoon light Karo
syrup

¼ cup cornstarch

2 cups fresh shredded
coconut

1 tablespoon butter

1 teaspoon almond extract

¼ cup heavy cream

AUNT MARIE'S COCONUT CAKE FILLING
VICTOR'S CAFETERIA
VICTOR AND CATHERINE C. HUCKABY, OWNERS
RECIPE COURTESY OF CATHERINE COURRÉGÉ HUCKABY

Marie Courrégé Rodrigue, the mother of George Rodrigue, was my aunt. My father, Emile Courrégé and Aunt Marie were two of eleven siblings. (My father was the tenth child; Aunt Marie was the "caboose," the eleventh child.) Aunt Marie lived walking distance from us, and as a child, I spent many hours at 1011 West St. Peter Street. It was there that George had his first studio in the attic, and the pulldown attic stairs were always left down so he could have easy access to his artwork. How many times I watched Aunt Marie gingerly climb those stairs to bring meals to her beloved son! As it turned out, George was not only a loving son, husband, and father, but also a loving cousin and friend. Full of humor, with his memorable laugh, and quick wit, to pass time with George was always rewarding. Aunt Marie's Coconut Cake Filling was like no other because she used a FRESH coconut!

Make a simple syrup. In a saucepan, stir together the sugar, ½ cup water, and the Karo syrup and bring to a boil, stirring until the sugar is dissolved.

Meanwhile, make a slurry. In a small bowl, combine the cornstarch and 2 tablespoons water, stirring until completely dissolved and smooth.

Add the slurry all at once to the hot simple syrup and stir until thickened. Remove the saucepan from the heat. Add the coconut, butter, and almond extract and stir until the butter has melted and the mixture is combined. Add the heavy cream and stir until all is incorporated.

Let the mixture cool to room temperature before using as a filling. If not using it right away, transfer the coconut filling to a bowl and keep it chilled, covered with plastic wrap, in the refrigerator. When ready to use, if you think it is too thick, heat it in the microwave for 20 seconds. Stir well.

RED VELVET CHEESECAKE
CHARLEY G'S
KAYLEE RATCLIFF, PASTRY CHEF

Lafayette ★

While some Louisiana restaurants serve savory versions of cheese-cake (even alligator or crab) as an entrée, Charley G's in Lafayette takes the sweet route for dessert with their red velvet cheesecake. Pastry Chef Kaylee Ratcliff's masterpiece uses buttermilk for an extra-thick and creamy texture, and chocolate cookie crumbs for a luscious chocolatey crust.

Make the chocolate crust. Preheat the oven to 400°F. Melt the butter in a small saucepan. In a small mixing bowl, mix together the butter with the cookie crumbs and sugar. Press into a 9-inch round springform pan or cake pan. Bake the crust for 7 minutes. Remove from oven and let cool.

Make the cheesecake batter. In the bowl of a stand mixer fitted with the paddle attachment, beat the cream cheese and sugar together until light and fluffy. In a mixing bowl, combine the buttermilk, cornstarch, lemon zest, lemon juice, vanilla extract, vinegar, and red food dye and slowly add to the cream cheese mixture. Finally, add the whole eggs, yolks, and cocoa powder and beat until incorporated.

When the crust is cool, pour the cheesecake batter into the pan. Bake for 10 minutes at 400°F, then reduce the heat to 200°F and bake for 30 minutes more. Remove the cheesecake from the oven and let it cool completely, about 4 hours, then refrigerate, for a minimum of 4 hours or overnight.

When the cheesecake has chilled completely, make the cream cheese frosting. In the bowl of the stand mixer fitted with the paddle attachment, beat the cream cheese and butter together until light and fluffy. Add the remaining frosting ingredients and beat until combined. Spread the cheesecake with the frosting and serve.

SERVES 8

FOR THE COOKIE CRUST

¼ cup butter

2 cups chocolate cookie crumbs

¼ cup sugar

FOR THE BATTER

3 cups cream cheese

1½ cups sugar

½ cup buttermilk

1 tablespoon cornstarch

1 teaspoon lemon zest

1 teaspoon lemon juice

1 teaspoon vanilla extract

1 teaspoon white distilled vinegar

1½ tablespoons red food dye

3 whole eggs

2 egg yolks

½ cup cocoa powder

FOR THE FROSTING

1 cup cream cheese

1 cup butter

3 cups powdered sugar

1 teaspoon vanilla extract

⅛ teaspoon salt

2 tablespoons lemon juice

Baton Rouge ★

SERVES 12

FOR THE BLUEBERRY SYRUP

2 cups frozen blueberries

1 cup sugar

3 tablespoons orange juice

FOR THE CHEESECAKE BATTER

2 pounds cream cheese, at room temperature

5¼ ounces (by weight) Danish blue cheese, at room temperature, or see Notes opposite

1⅓ cups sugar

4 eggs

FOR THE GINGER SNAP CRUST

14 ounces ginger snap cookies

½ teaspoon kosher salt

1 stick (½ cup) unsalted butter, melted

BLUE DOG BLUE CHEESECAKE WITH BLUEBERRY SWIRL AND GINGER SNAP CRUST
MANSURS ON THE BOULEVARD
BARRETT MEEKS, CHEF

This recipe comes from a wedding reception that Chef Barret Meeks attended at the New Orleans Museum of Art, way before he decided to cook professionally. Perhaps the champagne and great art had something to do with it, but it was a simple hors d'oeuvre—a ginger snap with some blue cheese and a blueberry on top—that inspired this cheesecake. The distinct flavors of the blue cheese and ginger snap with the sweetness of blueberries come together, much like Louisiana culture, to form a combination unlike anything else. Even people who claim to not like blue cheese are surprised by how much they enjoy this dessert.

Make the syrup. In a large saucepan, combine the blueberries, sugar, 1 cup of water, and the orange juice and bring to a simmer over medium heat. Let simmer for about 10 minutes, until reduced slightly. In a blender, blend mixture until smooth. Transfer syrup to another container and allow to cool completely.

Make the batter. In the bowl of a stand mixer fitted with the whisk attachment, whip together the cream cheese and blue cheese until blended. Add the sugar, whipping until blended, then continue to whip while adding the eggs, one at a time, until incorporated. Let rest in the refrigerator while finishing the other components.

Make the crust. In a food processor, add the ginger snaps and pulse until fine crumbs are formed. Transfer crumbs to a bowl, add the salt, and pour the melted butter over the crumbs. Stir the mixture until the crumbs hold their shape when you squeeze them in your hand.

Assemble and bake the cheesecake. Put the top oven rack in the middle position and preheat the oven to 200°F. Place a round piece of parchment in the bottom of a 10-inch spring-form pan and spray the bottom and sides with a non-stick cooking spray. Press the ginger snap crumbs into the bottom and halfway up the inside of the pan. (It's okay if you have some extra, it's better to have too much instead of not enough.)

Spoon in half of the cheesecake batter. Drizzle about one-third of the blueberry syrup in lines, back and forth over the top of the batter. Add the remaining batter on top and drizzle more of the syrup in lines, back and forth. Drag a knife through the batter to create a marbled effect. (If you have remaining syrup, you can drizzle it on top of the finished cake.)

Bake the cake in the center of the middle rack for an hour and twenty minutes, then increase heat to 250°F and bake for forty minutes more, or until set. Cool completely before cutting into slices. Garnish with any remaining blueberry syrup, if desired, or see Notes below.

Notes:
If you can't find a Danish blue cheese, you can use Gorgonzola, Roquefort, or Castello Blue.

To garnish, if you are feeling adventurous, you can dust slices of the cake with sugar and brûlée them with a torch.

NANCY SHI, *LOUISIANA SUPPER*, OIL/ACRYLIC (DETAIL) (FIRST PLACE JUNIOR)

New Orleans ★

SERVES 12

FOR THE STRAWBERRY BUTTERMILK SHERBET

¾ cup sugar

½ cup corn syrup

2¼ cups buttermilk

1¾ cups strawberry purée (see Pro Tip)

FOR THE MACERATED STRAWBERRIES

1 quart fresh strawberries, hulled

½ cup sugar

1 tablespoon cane vinegar

1 teaspoon vanilla extract

3 turns of freshly ground black pepper (about ¼ teaspoon)

FOR THE VANILLA CHANTILLY CREAM

1 cup heavy cream

3 tablespoons sugar

1 teaspoon vanilla extract

LOUISIANA WHOLE WHEAT STRAWBERRY SHORTCAKE

NEW ORLEANS CULINARY AND HOSPITALITY INSTITUTE (NOCHI)

ZAK MILLER, BAKING AND PASTRY ARTS INSTRUCTOR

NOCHI's accelerated six-month certificate program culminates with a pop-up café that's conceptualized and operated by students. Running the café serves as a capstone course and something of a "final exam" shortly before graduation. This recipe takes its inspiration from Hearth, the Winter 2022 cohort's concept. In Louisiana, we're lucky enough to have a winter strawberry season, and you can think of this as a more nuanced homage to the summery classic. Whole wheat imparts a nuttiness and warmth to the shortcakes, while buttermilk makes the sherbet tangy yet creamy.

Pro Tip: You'll need 1¾ cups of strawberry purée for the sherbet, made by simply puréeing and straining about 2 quarts of berries. Thawed frozen berries, however, work wonderfully, too.

Make the strawberry buttermilk sherbet. In a small saucepan, combine the sugar, ⅔ cup water, and the corn syrup over medium-high heat. Stir frequently and bring just to a boil to dissolve the sugar. Remove from the heat and transfer to a heatproof container. Refrigerate until chilled thoroughly.

When the syrup is thoroughly chilled, add the buttermilk and strawberry purée. Churn in an ice cream maker according to the manufacturer's instructions. Freeze for at least 4 hours, or until firm.

Make the macerated strawberries. Slice the strawberries about ⅛-inch thick. Combine with all remaining ingredients. Cover and refrigerate for at least 30 minutes. (The more time you give them to macerate, the more juice they will produce.)

Make the vanilla Chantilly cream. In a large bowl or the bowl of a stand mixer fitted with the whisk attachment, combine all ingredients and whip until stiff peaks form. Cover and keep refrigerated until you are ready to serve.

Make the shortcakes. In the bowl of a stand mixer fitted with the paddle attachment, combine the dry ingredients. Cut the cold butter into ½-inch pieces and add to the dry ingredients, mixing just until it's in pieces no larger than a pea. Add the cream, milk, and egg all at once. Mix until just combined, taking care not to overmix.

Dust a work surface with flour and turn the dough onto it. Dust the top of the dough and roll it to approximately ¾-inch thick. Use a floured 2-inch cutter to cut the dough into circles. If you'd like, you can gently combine and re-roll any scraps once (don't overwork the dough or it will get tough). Arrange the shortcakes on a baking sheet and refrigerate for 20 minutes.

Meanwhile, preheat the oven to 375°F (350°F with convection).

Before baking, brush the tops of the shortcakes with a bit of cream and sprinkle them with sugar. Bake for approximately 15 minutes, or until they are light golden brown. Allow to cool.

Assemble and serve the shortcakes. Split the shortcakes horizontally and top the bottom half with macerated strawberries, allowing their juice to soak into the cake. Top with a scoop of sherbet and garnish with Chantilly cream. Add the top of the shortcake and serve immediately.

FOR THE SHORTCAKES

¾ cup whole wheat flour

¾ cup all-purpose flour, plus more for rolling

⅓ cup sugar, plus more for baking

4 teaspoons baking powder

½ teaspoon kosher salt

½ cup (1 stick) cold unsalted butter

¼ cup heavy cream, plus more for baking

¼ cup whole milk

1 egg

Monroe

SERVES 6

FOR THE BREAD PUDDING

Butter, for coating baking dish

Sugar in the Raw, for coating baking dish

4 cups stale bread, cubed

2 cups milk

6 whole eggs

6 egg yolks

1 cup sugar

1 teaspoon vanilla

2 teaspoons cinnamon

1 teaspoon nutmeg

FOR THE BANANAS FOSTER SAUCE

1 stick (½ cup) unsalted butter

½ cup light brown sugar

2 bananas, sliced into rounds

¼ cup bourbon

Juice of one orange

1 teaspoon cinnamon

BANANAS FOSTER BREAD PUDDING
PARISH RESTAURANT
CORY BAHR, CHEF, OWNER, AND FOUNDER

Cory Bahr is the owner and founder of Parish Restaurant, Standard Coffee Co., and Heritage Catering in Monroe, Louisiana, where he was born and raised. Bread pudding is a Southern classic that has a special spot in everyone's heart. It's one of those foods that really shows how something amazing can be made from just a few basic ingredients. This recipe takes a fun spin on traditional bread pudding with another fan favorite: bananas foster. Easy to make and fun to eat, this dessert will be a hit no matter the audience!

Pro Tip: Coating the baking dish in butter and Sugar in the Raw adds even more flavor and a great texture to your bread pudding.

Make the bread pudding. Preheat the oven to 375°F. Butter a 16- by 9- by 2-inch (or 3 quart) casserole dish and coat the dish with Sugar in the Raw. Place the bread cubes in a large mixing bowl and set aside.

Pour the milk into a saucepan and bring to a low simmer over low heat. Meanwhile, whisk together the eggs, egg yolks, sugar, vanilla, cinnamon, and nutmeg in a bowl. When the milk is warm, slowly pour it into the egg mixture, whisking constantly, until fully incorporated.

Pour the custard over the reserved bread cubes, then gently fold until all the bread is evenly coated. Pour the bread mixture into the prepared baking dish and bake for 30 minutes, or until the bread pudding is a nice golden brown and has set in the center. Transfer to a cooling rack to cool 10 to 15 minutes while you prepare the sauce.

Make the sauce. Melt the butter in a saucepan over medium-high heat, then add the brown sugar and bananas and cook for a few minutes. Add the bourbon, then continue to cook, stirring occasionally, until the smell of alcohol dissipates. Add the orange juice and cinnamon, stirring to combine. Pour the sauce over the slightly cooled (but still warm) bread pudding.

SAVANNAH BRISTER, CATALYST, OIL/ACRYLIC

New Orleans ★

SERVES 18 TO 20

FOR THE BREAD AND CUSTARD MIXTURE

12 to 14 cups cubed dry French bread

8 whole eggs

8 egg yolks

¾ cup granulated sugar

1 tablespoon cinnamon

1 tablespoon ground nutmeg

2 quarts heavy cream

3 cups milk (may need a little more)

1 tablespoon good vanilla

¼ cup Calvados

FOR THE APPLE MIXTURE

3 sticks (¾ pound) unsalted butter, divided

1 cup packed brown sugar

¾ cup granulated sugar

2 tablespoons good vanilla

8 Granny Smith apples, peeled, cored, and sliced, reserving peels and cores for vanilla bean sauce

APPLE UPSIDE-DOWN BREAD PUDDING WITH VANILLA BEAN SAUCE
GABRIELLE RESTAURANT
MARY SONNIER, CHEF

Originally invented to use up leftover table bread, Apple Upside-Down Bread Pudding is one of the most popular desserts served at Gabrielle Restaurant. Cubes of French bread are layered on top of sliced apples and baked in a decadent boozy custard. Topped with vanilla bean sauce, a pan of this is a great way to feed a crowd.

Make the bread and custard mixture. Put the bread cubes in a large bowl. In a large mixing bowl, whisk together the whole eggs and yolks until well blended. In a small bowl mix together the sugar, cinnamon, and nutmeg. Slowly whisk the spiced sugar into the eggs and whisk until all the sugar is dissolved. Add the cream, milk (start with 3 cups and add more if necessary to soak the bread), vanilla, and Calvados and stir until well mixed. Pour the custard over the bread and soak 1 to 2 hours.

Prepare the apples and cook the bread pudding. Preheat the oven to 350°F. Melt 2 sticks (½ pound) of the butter in a skillet over low heat, then stir in the brown sugar, granulated sugar, and vanilla, stirring until the sugar is dissolved. Add the apples and sauté until the apples are softened, five to 8 minutes. Pour the apples into a large 13- by 9-inch baking pan, spreading them out evenly, then pour the chilled bread mixture over apples and stud with the remaining 1 stick (¼ pound) butter. Bake, covered, 90 minutes, then uncover and continue to bake until browned on top and a toothpick comes out clean, about 45 minutes more.

ISABELLA MAINIERO, *MARILYNN'S PLACE*, OTHER (DETAIL)

While the bread pudding bakes, make the vanilla bean sauce. Place the reserved apple peels and cores in a large saucepan, then add the sugar, vanilla beans, and enough water to cover the peels and cores. Bring the mixture to a simmer over low heat and continue to simmer until the sauce is reduced by half.

When the bread pudding is done, remove it from the oven and let cool slightly, then invert onto a sheet pan. To serve, ladle about 2 tablespoons of vanilla bean sauce onto each plate, top with a slice of warm pudding, and then whipped cream. Garnish with toasted and spiced nuts, if desired.

FOR THE VANILLA BEAN SAUCE

Reserved apple peels and cores (from making apple mixture)

1½ cups sugar

2 vanilla beans

Whipped cream, for serving

Toasted and spiced nuts, for garnish (optional)

Washington

MAKES 24 COOKIES

FOR THE DOUGH

2½ cups all-purpose flour

1½ cups cake flour

2 teaspoons cornstarch

2 teaspoons ground cinnamon

1 teaspoon baking powder

1 teaspoon baking soda

1 teaspoon salt

½ cup (1 stick) cold unsalted butter, cubed

1 cup light brown sugar, packed

½ cup granulated sugar

2 large whole eggs

2 large egg yolks

2 teaspoons vanilla extract

1 teaspoon almond extract

FOR THE CINNAMON SUGAR TOPPING

4 tablespoons granulated sugar

2 teaspoons ground cinnamon

KING CAKE COOKIES
WASHINGTON CAREER AND TECHNICAL EDUCATION CENTER
AMANDA WILDBLOOD, PROSTART EDUCATOR

Everyone loves King Cake, and most Louisianans would love to have it year-round if they could. ProStart Educator Amanda Wildblood brought the dream to life, in cookie form, for her ProStart students. Sweet sugar cookies, topped with cinnamon and a Carnival-colored special glaze, will give you the Mardi Gras spirit anytime of the year!

Make the dough. Preheat the oven to 400°F. Whisk together the all-purpose flour, cake flour, cornstarch, cinnamon, baking powder, baking soda, and salt in a large bowl. Set aside.

Place the cold, cubed butter into the bowl of a stand mixer and secure the paddle attachment. Turn the mixer on the lowest setting and cream the butter for 30 seconds, then add in the brown sugar and mix for 30 seconds, followed by the granulated sugar for 30 seconds, or until light and fluffy. Add in the eggs, egg yolks, vanilla extract, and almond extract and blend until combined. If any of the butter gets stuck on the paddle attachment, stop the mixer and use a rubber spatula to knock it off. Keeping the mixer on low speed, gradually add in the reserved flour mixture, about ¼ cup at a time, until incorporated.

Make the cinnamon sugar topping. In a small bowl, stir together the sugar and cinnamon. Set aside.

Form and bake the cookies. Measure out about 2¼ tablespoons of dough and form into balls that are nice and tall (don't flatten them). Roll the dough balls in the cinnamon sugar mixture and place on a cookie sheet, about 1 inch apart. (You can use a silicone baking mat or parchment paper if you prefer.) Bake for 10 to 11 minutes (depending on oven), or until lightly brown on the edges. (The secret is to pull the cookies out of the oven before you think they are done. They will seem gooey in the center, but they are fully cooked.) Let cookies rest on the sheet for 15 minutes, then transfer them to a cooling rack to cool completely.

As the cookies cool, make the glaze. In a shallow bowl, stir together the confectioners' sugar, butter, vanilla extract, and almond extract. Add the food coloring, if using. (If you'd like to make several different colors, divide the confectioners' sugar mixture into individual bowls before adding the food coloring of choice.) Add 1 tablespoon of the milk and stir to make a thick glaze, then slowly stir in enough of the remaining tablespoon of milk until you reach the desired consistency. (If you are making several different glaze colors, add just enough milk to each bowl until you reach the desired consistency.)

When the cookies are cool, dip them, one at a time, into the glaze and decorate, as desired. The glaze will form a crust and harden as it cools. If needed, you can warm glaze during dipping process.

SHANIA RAIMER, *I GOT DA BABY!,* OTHER

FOR THE GLAZE

4 cups confectioners' sugar

4 tablespoons butter, softened

2 teaspoons vanilla extract, clear

1 teaspoon almond extract

Purple, green, or gold food coloring (optional)

1 to 2 tablespoons milk

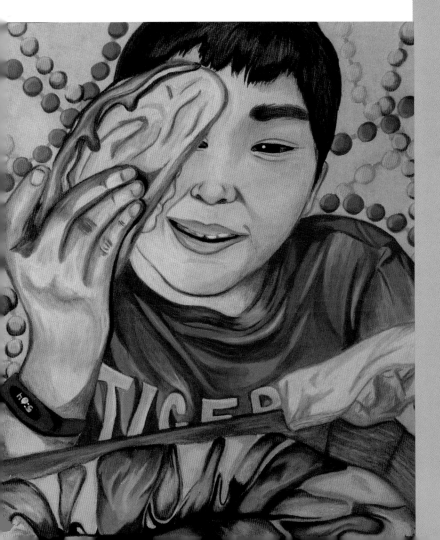

Lake Charles
★

SERVES 14

FOR THE ICE CREAM BASE

3 cups heavy whipping cream

1 cup whole milk

9 large egg yolks

¾ cup plus 3 tablespoons granulated sugar

Pinch of salt

FOR THE LEMON CURD

9 large egg yolks

1¼ cups plus 1 tablespoon granulated sugar

Pinch of salt

¾ cup freshly squeezed lemon juice, strained

1 stick (8 tablespoons) butter, diced, at room temperature

FOR THE SWISS MERINGUE

4 large egg whites

1 cup granulated sugar

LEMON GELATO
LA TRUFFE SAUVAGE
MOHAMED CHETTOUH AND ARTHUR DURHAM, CHEFS/OWNERS

Years ago, Chef Mohamed Chettouh, lead chef at La Truffe Sauvage, was in France and came upon a gelato vendor who sold lemon gelato topped with Italian meringue. He was so taken by it that he decided to replicate it for the restaurant. Now it's a challenge to make sure they always have enough on hand for their guests. In classical cuisine, meringues have several different classifications, which indicate the way the meringue is prepared. At La Truffe Sauvage, a Swiss meringue, probably the easiest, is used. It certainly works well for their operation, and it will work well in your kitchen, too. This recipe is a great way to use egg yolks, and it leaves you with so many egg whites, you can make soufflés, without letting anything go to waste!

Make the ice cream base. Place the cream and milk in a heavy, non-aluminum/nonreactive 1½- to 2-quart saucepan and place over medium heat. Combine the egg yolks, sugar, and salt in a mixing bowl and whisk until smooth. Increase the heat for the dairy mixture and bring to a boil, then reduce heat to medium. Pour half of the hot dairy mixture into the bowl with the egg mixture, stir until smooth, then return to the saucepan, whisking constantly to prevent scorching, and continue to cook until the mixture reaches 180°F. Immediately transfer the ice cream base to a container and place in an ice bath to stop the cooking and chill. (Or you can place the pan in an ice water bath to stop the cooking and chill). Once chilled, transfer to the refrigerator and let chill about 2 hours, until very cold.

Make the lemon curd. In a heavy, non-aluminum/reactive saucepan, combine the egg yolks, sugar, and salt and whisk until smooth. Add the lemon juice, stir until smooth, then add all the diced butter. Heat the mixture over medium heat (not too high or mixture will scorch), whisking constantly and paying careful attention to scrape the bottom and sides of the saucepan, until the mixture reaches 180°F, then immediately strain into a container. (As the mixture approaches 180°F, it will resemble a thick hollandaise.)

Finish the gelato mixture and freeze. Combine the lemon curd and ice cream base (which can be done while either is still warm), then transfer to a container and place in an ice bath until cold. Once chilled, it can be stored in the refrigerator or immediately put in an ice cream maker to be churned. Freeze according to ice cream maker's instructions.

While the gelato freezes, make the Swiss meringue. Combine the egg whites and sugar, preferably in the mixing bowl of a stand mixer (or, if whisking by hand, in a metal mixing bowl), and whisk well. Place the mixing bowl over a saucepan filled with hot water and stir constantly until mixture is warm (like a warm bath.) Transfer, if needed, to the mixing bowl of a stand mixer fitted with a whip attachment and whip on high speed until thick and light, about 5 minutes. Use immediately or keep in the freezer until ready to use (see Note).

To serve, scoop ½ cup of the gelato into a small dessert bowl and then add a dollop of the meringue on top. If a torch is available, lightly toasting the meringue adds to the enjoyment.

Note:
The meringue can be made ahead of time and kept frozen for up to 4 days.

New Orleans ★

MAKES 24 SQUARES

FOR THE CRUST

6 tablespoons unsalted butter

4 tablespoons sugar

1 egg, beaten

4 tablespoons milk

2 cups all-purpose flour

¼ teaspoon salt

FOR THE SWEET POTATO FILLING

2 cups fresh sweet potato, cooked, peeled, and lightly mashed

2 tablespoons unsalted butter, melted

2 tablespoons vanilla extract

½ cup Chef Paul Prudhomme's Sweetie Magic®

⅛ teaspoon salt

1 egg, beaten

2 tablespoons heavy cream

2 tablespoons sugar

SWEET POTATO PECAN PIE SQUARES WITH CHANTILLY CREAM
MAGIC SEASONING BLENDS
CHEF PAUL PRUDHOMME

Chef Paul's hometown, Opelousas, Louisiana, is the Sweet Potato Capital of the World. For many years, at the end of the harvest, a week was devoted to a festival, called Yambilee. One of Chef's vivid memories of Yambilee was literally the hundreds of ways that sweet potato can be cooked! This recipe, by far, was one of his all-time favorite sweet potato-eating experiences.

Make the crust. In a mixing bowl, cream the butter and sugar until light and fluffy. Add the egg and milk and beat for another 2 minutes. Stir the flour and salt into the wet mixture to form a dough. Turn out onto a lightly floured work surface and shape into a disk. Tightly wrap with plastic wrap and refrigerate at least 4 hours and up to 24 hours.

On a lightly floured work surface, roll the dough out to a 10 x 14-inch rectangle. Transfer to a 9- by 13-inch glass baking dish. Press pastry into dish and flute edges, then set aside.

Preheat the oven to 325°F.

Make the sweet potato filling. In a mixing bowl, combine all the sweet potato filling ingredients and beat at medium speed until mixture is smooth. Spread on bottom of pie crust.

Make the pecan filling. In a bowl, combine all the pecan filling ingredients and mix well. Pour over sweet potato filling.

Bake the pie in the oven for 55 to 60 minutes, or until toothpick comes out clean. Remove from oven and cool on a wire rack. To serve, slice into 24 pieces, and serve with a dollop of Chantilly cream (recipe follows).

Note:
To freeze, let pie cool completely, then refrigerate for 24 hours. Cut into bars, and individually wrap with plastic wrap. Freeze for up to 1 month. To defrost, simply remove bars from freezer and thaw in refrigerator.

ALEXIS ADAMS, PAUL PRUDHOMME, MIXED MEDIA

CHANTILLY CREAM

Refrigerate a mixing bowl and beaters until very cold. Combine the cream, vanilla, brandy, and Grand Marnier in the mixing bowl and beat on medium speed for 1 minute. Add the sugar and sour cream and beat on medium speed just until soft peaks form, about 3 minutes. Do not overbeat. (Overbeating will make the cream grainy, which is the first step leading to butter. Once grainy you can't return it to its former consistency, but if this ever happens, enjoy it on toast!)

FOR THE PECAN FILLING

¾ cup pecans, chopped

¾ cup pecans, halved

1½ cups sugar

4 eggs

3 tablespoons unsalted butter, melted

1½ cups dark corn syrup

⅛ teaspoon salt

½ teaspoon cinnamon

1 tablespoon vanilla extract

FOR THE CHANTILLY CREAM

MAKES ABOUT 2 CUPS

⅔ cup heavy cream

1 teaspoon vanilla extract

1 teaspoon brandy

1 teaspoon Grand Marnier

¼ cup sugar

2 tablespoons dairy sour cream

Chalmette ★

SERVES 6

FOR THE APPLE FILLING

1 large apple, cut into small chunks

1 tablespoon unsalted butter, cubed

1 tablespoon brown sugar

¼ teaspoon cinnamon

⅛ teaspoon cardamom

¼ cup sparkling apple cider

1 sheet gelatin

FOR THE CRUST

¼ cup graham cracker crumbs

1 tablespoon brown sugar

1 tablespoon oatmeal

2 tablespoons pecan flour

2 tablespoons unsalted butter, melted

FOR THE SALTED CARAMEL

¼ cup granulated sugar

½ cup heavy whipping cream, at room temperature

2 tablespoons unsalted butter

¼ teaspoon salt

APPLE CRISP DOME WITH FRESH FRUIT, SALTED CARAMEL, AND CHANTILLY WHIPPED CREAM

CHALMETTE HIGH SCHOOL
ELENA HODGES, PROSTART EDUCATOR AND CHEF

This dessert, from the ProStart class at Chalmette High School and winners of our 2022 Raising Cane's Chicken Fingers Louisiana ProStart Invitational, showcases many familiar flavors, and perhaps one that's not quite so familiar—cardamom. With its subtle, menthol-like flavor, this spice adds something pleasantly unexpected to this fruity dessert. Native to South India, the spice comes from the cardamom plant, a relative of ginger and turmeric. You've most likely tasted cardamom in a chai latte, and now you can try a new flavor in this award-winning desert.

Make the apple filling. In a 2-quart saucepan add the apple, butter, brown sugar, cinnamon, cardamom, and apple cider and bring mixture to a boil over medium heat, then reduce heat to low and continue to cook until the apples are soft. Add the gelatin sheet and stir until it is fully dissolved. Put the filling in a half sphere silicone mold or divide filling among a six-cavity mold and refrigerate until set, about 45 minutes.

Meanwhile, make the crust. Add the graham cracker crumbs, sugar, oatmeal, and pecan flour to a medium-size bowl and stir to combine. Add the melted butter and mix until the crust resembles wet sand. Press crust mixture into the half sphere mold or into six 2-inch ring molds, and place in refrigerator to set.

When the apple filling is set and the crust is set, assemble the crisp. Unmold the crust from the ring mold. Carefully remove the half sphere of apple mold and place on the crust. (If you are using the six-cavity mold for the apple filling, carefully remove the smaller half spheres of apple from the mold and place each on a crust.)

ANGEL WILLIAMS, *PLATED CULTURE*, OIL/ACRYLIC

Make the salted caramel. In a heavy-bottomed saucepan melt the sugar over medium-low heat. When the sugar turns a golden amber color, remove from heat. Add in the heavy cream, butter, and salt. Stir to combine.

Make the Chantilly whipped cream. In a large mixing bowl, add the mascarpone cheese and whip until smooth. Add the heavy whipping cream, powdered sugar, and vanilla. Beat until stiff peaks form. Do not overmix.

To plate, sprinkle the crumbs of a crushed meringue cookie on the side of each serving dish in a crescent pattern. Place unmolded apple dome and crust in the middle of the crescent. Garnish with the Chantilly cream, fruit, and small mint leaves. Drizzle the top with the salted caramel.

FOR THE CHANTILLY WHIPPED CREAM

¼ cup mascarpone cheese

½ cup heavy whipping cream, chilled

1 tablespoon powdered sugar

1 teaspoon vanilla extract

FOR THE GARNISH

6 meringue cookies, crushed

6 strawberries

12 raspberries

12 blackberries

1½ kiwis, cut into slices, then quartered

About 18 small mint leaves, to taste

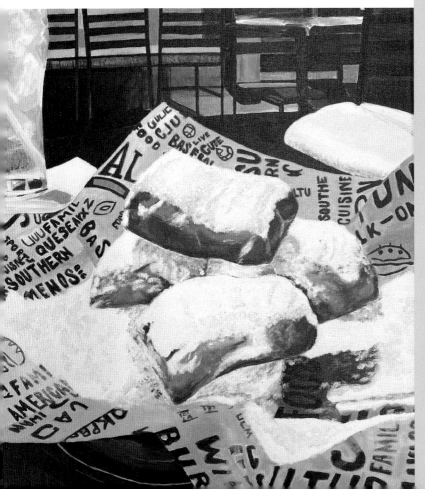

Leesville ★

3 ripe bananas

½ cup (1 stick) butter, softened

¾ cup sugar

2 cups flour

1 teaspoon baking soda

½ teaspoon salt

HAZEL'S BANANA BREAD
HAZEL'S TEA PARLOR
DONNA ROARK, CHEF
MARGARET MATTHEWS, OWNER
RON MATTHEWS II, MANAGER

Located in Vernon Parish Louisiana, Hazel's Tea Parlor is situated in a lovely one-story Victorian home. When you visit, you'll have the option of dining in Sofia's Dining Room or relaxing in Chloe's Parlor. Soups, sandwiches, salads, desserts and, of course, a large variety of hot teas are elegantly served.

Preheat the oven to 350°F. Grease only the bottom of a loaf pan. In a large mixing bowl, mash the bananas, then add the softened butter and sugar and cream well. Add the flour, baking soda, and salt and hand-mix until blended. Transfer the mixture to the prepared loaf pan, smoothing the top.

Place the loaf in the oven and bake for 45 to 60 minutes. Let cool for 5 minutes, then remove from the pan.

IAN PENA, *DONNER LE DULCE,* WATERCOLOR

CHAPTER SEVEN
COCKTAILS AND DRINKS

New Orleans ★

SERVES 1

Handful of fresh mint
leaves

½ ounce mint syrup, or
more to taste (see Note), or
simple syrup

3 ounces Old Soul
Bourbon, divided

Smacked mint sprig, for
garnish

MINT JULEP
STAR CRAFT NOLA COCKTAILS AND ELIXIRS
STAR HODGSON, MIXOLOGIST

There probably is no cocktail more quintessentially Southern than the Mint Julep. While the drink was first mentioned in print circa 1803, it evolved over that century into the cocktail we know today. Mostly found in big city hotel bars that had access to ice blocks, the Julep was considered to be the most civilized way to drink the sometimes harsh corn whiskeys of the era. The use of crushed ice in this drink is crucial, since we start with a high proof bourbon that evolves slowly as you sip from the dilution, as it occurs. This is what I call a start-to-finish drink.

ProTip: Using a metal Julep cup with a metal straw will keep your Mint Julep icy-cold. (And your effort will look professional, too!)

Lightly bruise your mint leaves by squeezing them in your hand to get the oils flowing, then place them in the bottom of your cup (preferably a metal Julep cup with a metal straw). Add the mint syrup and 2 ounces of the bourbon, then lightly stir with the mint before filling your cup with crushed ice, packing it in tightly. Top with the remaining ounce of bourbon, then use the metal straw to create a space down the side of the cup to place your smacked mint sprig. Sip slowly and savor the evolution of flavors.

Note:
To make the mint syrup, remove bottom leaves from mint sprigs, reserving the tops for garnishes. Add about a cup of mint leaves (no stems, they become bitter) to a 4-cup container. Add 2 cups of sugar and stir the leaves to coat. Allow to rest for 30 minutes, then add 1 cup warm (not hot) water to the sugar and stir to dissolve. Add 1 cup ice water and stir again before straining into another vessel, such as a flip-top glass bottle or whatever you have on hand. The mint syrup will keep at least 2 weeks when refrigerated, and longer if you add an ounce of vodka.

CAPITAL COCKTAIL
THE BOURBON SOCIETY OF BATON ROUGE
AARON BERTRAND, DRINK CREATOR AND WINNER OF THE LOUISIANA BOURBON FESTIVAL COCKTAIL CONTEST

Baton Rouge ★

To commemorate its 50th year in 2022, Visit Baton Rouge introduced this cocktail to keep the celebration of promoting Louisiana's capital city alive for many years to come. Created by Aaron Bertrand of the Bourbon Society of Baton Rouge, the Capital Cocktail is a bourbon-based drink that ties in a taste of Baton Rouge by using Louisiana molasses and honey.

Using a condiment dispenser (or squeeze bottle), spread the honey/molasses blend in a striped pattern around the inside of a cocktail glass.

Muddle 1 blackberry in the bottom of the glass, then fill glass with crushed ice. Set aside.

In a cocktail shaker with ice, blend the bourbon, simple syrup, lemon juice, and orange bitters. Shake and strain into a glass.

If desired, smoke briefly with the smoking wood. Garnish with a lemon blackberry twist and the remaining 2 blackberries. Enjoy responsibly!

SERVES 1

50/50 blend of honey and blackstrap molasses

3 blackberries (1 for muddle, 2 for garnish)

2½ ounces bourbon

½ to ¾ ounce honey, lemon, or ginger simple syrup (depending on bourbon proof)

½ to ¾ ounce freshly squeezed lemon juice

2 dashes orange bitters

Fruit-based smoking wood (preferably cherry or pear), optional

Lemon blackberry twist, for garnish

GOSPEL BIRD
CHICKEN AND CHAMPAGNE
DENISEEA TAYLOR, FOUNDER/MIXOLOGIST

New Orleans ★

This libation is in honor of the Gospel Bird, aka Fried Chicken, and to mixologist Deniseea Taylor there is no better pairing. To her mind, fried chicken, once a complex dish only enjoyed on special occasions, should always be celebrated, sort of like Champagne. The history of fried chicken, as it relates to the South and Black entrepreneurship after the Civil War, can only be celebrated with bubbles.

Chill a coupe glass. Add all ingredients, except the champagne, to a shaker with ice. Shake and strain into the chilled glass.

Top with the Champagne. Pair with your favorite piece of fried chicken. (P.S. You get extra credit if you fry the chicken yourself!)

SERVES 1

1 ounce passion fruit purée

¾ ounce caramel syrup

½ ounce fresh lime juice

Moët & Chandon Imperial Brut

MARY-EVELYN KING, *MEREDITH MEETS MUDBUG*, MIXED MEDIA
(FOURTH PLACE SENIOR)

New Orleans

SERVES 1

1 ounce Hennessy V.S.O.P. Cognac

½ ounce plantain syrup (recipe follows)

½ ounce fresh lemon juice

Pinch of sea salt

Moët & Chandon Imperial Brut

FOR THE PLANTAIN SYRUP

1 semi-black, soft plantain, cut into ½-inch round slices

1 teaspoon butter

2 cups sugar

PURR
CHICKEN AND CHAMPAGNE
DENISEEA TAYLOR, FOUNDER/MIXOLOGIST

This cocktail from mixologist Deniseea Taylor is a riff on a French 75. It reminds her of the beloved Bananas Foster, but highlights plantains instead. She's often inspired by history when creating cocktails, and the New Orleans history of the banana trade—the docks of New Orleans were once bustling with fruit, including bananas—was her main inspiration for this recipe.

Put all ingredients, except the Champagne, into a shaker with ice. Shake vigorously for 15 seconds, then double-strain into a coupe glass.

Top with the Champagne, sip, repeat.

PLANTAIN SYRUP

In a skillet, fry the plantain in the butter until golden on both sides.

In a small pot, bring 1 cup water to a boil, then stir in the sugar. Once the sugar is dissolved, add the plantains. Remove from heat and allow to rest for up to 48 hours.

LILY NI, *IT TAKES BERRIES TO MAKE JAM*, OTHER (SECOND PLACE SENIOR)

ESPRESSO MARTINI
MILK PUNCH MEDIA
MELISSA TOWNSEND, MIXOLOGIST

Variations of this 80's classic abound around New Orleans. This home bar version sticks close to the original with added chocolate and vanilla flavors.

Add all ingredients to a shaker filled with ice and give it a good hard shake. Strain into a martini or coupe glass.

Garnish with 3 whole coffee beans, representing health, wealth, and happiness. Cheers!

New Orleans ★

SERVES 1

1½ ounces vodka

1½ ounces fresh-brewed espresso or Cold Brew Concentrate

½ ounce coffee liqueur

½ ounce Tempus Fugit Crème de Cacao

3 coffee beans, for garnish

New Orleans ★

64 ounces tomato juice or Bloody Mary mix

1 fifth vodka (such as J.T. Meleck)

1 cup olive juice

½ cup Worcestershire sauce

4 tablespoons prepared horseradish sauce

6 to 8 dashes Tabasco sauce or Louisiana Hot Sauce

Juice of 2 lemons or limes

Garnishes, as desired

BLOODY MARY
MILK PUNCH MEDIA
MELISSA TOWNSEND, MIXOLOGIST

From Mardi Gras to Saints gameday season, everyone needs a go-to "Hair of the Blue Dog" bloody!

Combine all ingredients in a glass container and stir to combine. Cover and chill.

Serve over ice and with a DIY garnish bar.

THE AMELIE
CAFÉ AMELIE
STAR CRAFT NOLA COCKTAILS AND ELIXIRS
STAR HODGSON, MIXOLOGIST

New Orleans ★

Nestled in the heart of the French Quarter lies a lush secret court-yard, fragrant with the scent of orange blossom. For 16 years, locals and visitors alike have been dining and celebrating at this gem of hospitality. The signature namesake cocktail has remained a staple over the years. Bursting with flavors of fresh mint and lime, it's the perfect summer refreshment for enjoying an afternoon under the trees.

Prepare the rim of a tall glass, if desired: Rub the top of your glass with the lime wedge and then dip the rim into the sugar.

Lightly squeeze a palmful of mint and place it in the prepared glass, if using, or any tall glass. Add the Belvedere vodka, mint syrup, lime juice, and still or sparkling water, then fill with crushed ice. Garnish with a smacked sprig of mint.

Note:
To make the mint syrup, remove bottom leaves from mint sprigs, reserving the tops for garnishes. Add about a cup of mint leaves (no stems, they become bitter) to a 4-cup container. Add 2 cups of sugar and stir the leaves to coat. Allow to rest for 30 minutes, then add 1 cup warm (not hot) water to the sugar and stir to dissolve. Add 1 cup ice water and stir again before straining into another vessel, such as a flip-top glass bottle or whatever you have on hand. The mint syrup will keep at least 2 weeks when refrigerated, and longer if you add an ounce of vodka.

SERVES 1

1 lime wedge, to moisten rim of glass (optional)

Sugar, to rim the glass (optional)

Palmful of mint leaves

2 ounces Belvedere Vodka

1 ounce fresh mint syrup (see Note)

¾ ounce fresh lime juice

¾ ounce still or sparkling water

Smacked sprig of mint, for garnish

ANNA MILLER, *SHRIMP AND OKRA GUMBO, DIGITAL MEDIA*

New Orleans ★

SERVES 1

1 ounce Gravier Gin

2 ounces Butterfly Lavender Essence (see Note)

¾ ounce lemon juice

1½ ounces Chandon Brut Sparkling

Lavender petal-dusted lemon wheel, for garnish

LAVENDER FIELDS
STAR CRAFT NOLA COCKTAILS AND ELIXIRS
STAR HODGSON, MIXOLOGIST

Each March, the promise of a long, beautiful spring season arrives, as we tell ourselves, "This is the weather we overlook the muggy eternal summers for." As the flowers bloom, the perfume of night blooming jasmine fills the air, and centuries-old oak trees burst with lime-green buds, shading the streets with their long spidery branches.

Add the gin, butterfly lavender essence, and lemon juice to a mixing tin with ice and shake for 20 seconds (or until tin becomes a bit frosty). Strain into a coupe glass (or champagne flute) and top with the Chandon Brut. Garnish with a lemon wheel dipped in lavender petals.

Note:
To make butterfly lavender essence: Take 8 Butterfly Pea flowers and 1 tablespoon of dried organic lavender flowers and steep in ½ cup boiling water for 5 minutes. Strain flowers and add ½ cup sugar, stir to dissolve, and finish with 2 cups cold water. May be refrigerated for up to 2 weeks.

BATCHED SAZERACS
MILK PUNCH MEDIA
MELISSA TOWNSEND, MIXOLOGIST

New Orleans
★

The Sazerac House in New Orleans tells the incredible backstory of the components that make up a true Sazerac cocktail: Herbsaint Liqueur and Peychaud's Bitters. Together they complete the drink's storied history and bless this deep cherry-hued sipper with a unique blend of aromatics. Although the drink is stirred, you can batch Sazeracs for parties with impressive results. Have an atomizer handy to spray the essence of Herbsaint inside your glasses, or simply swirl some of the liqueur inside each chilled glass and then discard it.

Combine the rye, simple syrup, and 1¼ cups water in a large container. Funnel this base mixture into empty liquor bottles and chill.

Chill rocks glasses.

To serve 1 Sazerac, spray a chilled rocks glass with the Herbsaint. Add the Peychaud's Bitters. Pour about 2½ ounces chilled base mixture into the glass. Express a lemon peel over the drink and drop it into the glass.

Note:
To make rich simple syrup, dissolve 1 cup sugar in ½ cup hot water. Cool before using.

SERVES 12

3 cups Sazerac Rye Whiskey

3 ounces rich simple syrup (2:1, see Note)

Herbsaint Liqueur, for spraying glasses

5 dashes Peychaud's Bitters

Lemon peels, for garnish

New Orleans ★

SERVES 1

1½ ounce X by Glenmorangie single malt whiskey

1 ounce cinnamon-infused apple cider (see Note)

½ ounce ginger liqueur (such as Giffard Ginger of the Indies)

¼ ounce lemon juice

Cinnamon-dusted apple slice, for garnish (see Note)

WINTER IS COMING
STAR CRAFT NOLA COCKTAILS AND ELIXIRS
STAR HODGSON, MIXOLOGIST

Sometimes it gets cold here, and sometimes it gets really, really cold. Those are the days when we switch our spirits from clear to dark and bust out the winter coats. After a few sips, you will feel your soul warm up and your toes tingle.

In a mixing glass, add all ingredients, fill with ice, and stir for 30 rotations. Strain into a rocks glass over fresh ice, and garnish with a cinnamon-dusted apple slice.

Notes:
To infuse apple cider with cinnamon, just drop one cinnamon stick into a jug of cider. The flavors will develop over the course of 12 to 24 hours. If needed sooner, you can simmer the cider with a few sticks, then cool and use.

To keep apple slices from browning, dip them into lemon juice immediately after slicing.

THE NORTHERNMOST ISLAND IN THE CARIBBEAN
STAR CRAFT NOLA COCKTAILS AND ELIXIRS
STAR HODGSON, MIXOLOGIST

New Orleans

Notes of sweet and savory, tangy and tart, bitter and spice meld in this cocktail, reminiscent of the flavors and cultures of the Caribbean and our multicultural melting-pot here in New Orleans. Long considered the northernmost island in the Caribbean, Nola is known for its joyous and colorful celebrations of life, death, and all the many moments in-between.

Add the aged rum, basil-infused pineapple juice, and passionfruit pulp to a tall glass. Fill with ice, then garnish with the smacked basil sprig and top with several dashes of Angostura bitters.

Note:
The basil will infuse into the pineapple juice in as little as 30 minutes. Remove the stems to hinder bitterness.

SERVES 1

2 ounces aged rum, such as Don Q Reserva 7 Rum

3 ounces basil-infused pineapple juice (See Note)

½ ounce unsweetened passionfruit pulp, such as Goya

Smacked basil sprig, for garnish

Several dashes Angostura Bitters, to float

KENZI PERTUIT, *HUNGER PAINS,* MIXED MEDIA (DETAIL)

New Orleans ★

½ ounce lime juice

¼ ounce agave nectar, or simple syrup

2 ounces Blanco Tequila (such as Lunazul)

1½ ounces brewed unsweetened hibiscus tea, cooled

1 ounce coconut water

Dash of Tajín, or other chili-lime spice

Large format ice cube (optional)

Tajín-dusted lime wheel, for garnish

I LEFT MY HEART IN JALISCO
STAR CRAFT NOLA COCKTAILS AND ELIXIRS
STAR HODGSON, MIXOLOGIST

The tropical flavors of hibiscus tea and coconut water work in tandem with the vegetal nature of the tequila and the spice of the chili in this cocktail, making it a summertime soother for all climates, at any latitude.

Add the lime juice and agave nectar to a rocks glass and stir a few times to incorporate. Add the remaining ingredients, as well as the large format ice cube (or regular cubes), stir again, and garnish with a Tajín-dusted lime wheel.

SWEET TOOTH

These cavities
They rot my teeth
Like poison too me
With candy
You are my source of caffeine
Like coffee to my sugar
Your my In-between

I used to walk by your side
When we would walk
   through the lines
And I just thought
That this gumdrop boy
   has to be mine
But when my teeth start
   to rot
With the sugar that he's got
I just thought

He's got a sweet tooth
Maybe I'm bitter
Cause when I kiss him
He just starts to shiver
He's got a sweet tooth
   I'm just sour
Cause I make him pucker
And he starts to cower
Cause Baby I must be so sour
Ooooooooo
Baby I must be so sour

Sugar and spice
Everything nice
But this gumdrop boy
Needs some tart in his life
Cause he's just so sweet
And I guess I'm sour
He's making me rot,
   I have no power
I used to walk by your side

When we would walk
   through the lines
And I just thought
That this gumdrop boy
   has to be mine
But when my teeth start
   to rot
With the sugar that he's got
I just thought

He's got a sweet tooth
Maybe I'm bitter
Cause when I kiss him
He just starts to shiver
He's got a sweet tooth
I'm just sour
Cause I make him pucker
He starts to cower
Cause I just must
Be so sour
Ooooooooo
Baby am I just so sour

He's just a boy and I'm just
   a girl
But gumdrop boys don't fall
For lemon drop girls
Cause when he says my name
My teeth start to shiver
What's even the point
When we can't be together

I used to walk by your side
When we would walk
   through the lines
And I just thought
That this gumdrop boy
   has to be mine
But when my teeth start
   to rot
With the sugar that he's got
I just thought

He's got a sweet tooth
Maybe I'm bitter
Cause when I kiss him
He just starts to shiver
He's got a sweet tooth
I'm just sour
Cause I make him pucker
And he starts to cower
Cause I just must
Be so sour
Ooooooo
Baby am I just that sour

EMMA NAVARRO, SWEET TOOTH, THIRD PLACE WINNER - SONGWRITING CONTEST,
NEW ORLEANS CENTER FOR CREATIVE ARTS, NEW ORLEANS

New Orleans
★

SERVES 12 TO 15

1 envelope unflavored gelatin

¼ cup agave nectar

½ cup blanco tequila

¼ cup mezcal

¼ cup blue Curaçao

¼ cup fresh-squeezed lime juice

Sprinkle of salt

A few pomegranate seeds, plus more for garnish

Rosemary sprigs, for garnish

BLUE DOG MEZCAL MARGARITA GELATIN SHOTS
MILK PUNCH MEDIA
MELISSA TOWNSEND, MIXOLOGIST

These easy, make-ahead Blue Dog Mezcal Margarita Gelatin Shots are guaranteed to make everyone merry and will essentially rock the party! Mixologist Melissa Townsend makes them like a craft cocktail—all-natural with unflavored gelatin and fresh-squeezed lime (never lime-flavored Jell-O!) and with quality spirits—Espolòn Tequila Blanco; an approachable and not terribly aggressive mezcal (Montelobos or Ilegal Joven); and Giffard Blue Curaçao. The mezcal adds depth and warmth, with its smokiness, and the deep Caribbean-blue hue of the Curaçao is simply dreamy.

In a medium bowl, sprinkle the gelatin over 1 cup boiling water and whisk until smooth. Add the agave nectar and stir until combined. Allow to cool slightly and transfer to a glass measuring cup or small pitcher. Add the tequila, mezcal, blue Curaçao, and lime juice. Stir to combine.

Pour mixture into shot glasses. Sprinkle a little salt into each shot. Sprinkle a little salt and drop a few pomegranate seeds into each shot.

Chill at least 8 hours or overnight. To serve, garnish with more pomegranate seeds. Remove leaves from bottom half of rosemary sprigs and stick a sprig in each gelatin shot.

PJ'S WORLD-FAMOUS COLD BREW COFFEE
PJ'S COFFEE
PHYLLIS JORDAN, FOUNDER

New Orleans

Founded in 1978 by New Orleanian Phyllis Jordan, PJ's Coffee has become nationally known for using the top one percent of Arabica coffee beans, the most popular type of coffee in the world, originating in Ethiopia. Coffee enthusiasts enjoy a unique experience at each of PJ's Coffee shops, but this recipe for the brand's famous cold brew lets everyone enjoy the same experience in the comfort of their own home. An essential hot tip: make sure the coffee is coarsely ground!

Using a Toddy Cold Brew System (available at any PJ's café), pour the coffee into the steeping vessel and fill with room-temperature water. Steep for 14 hours.

Drain the coffee mixture into the glass decanter. Add ½ gallon filtered water and the vanilla. For one serving, pour desired amount of coffee over ice in a glass and add milk to desired preference.

SERVES 6

1 pound PJ's Viennese Blend Coffee, coarsely ground

Filtered Water

2 teaspoons Ronald Reginald's Melipone Mexican Vanilla (or any Mexican vanilla)

Milk, as desired

New Orleans ★

2 ounces raspberries

2 ounces bananas, frozen

2 ounces açaí purée, frozen

2 ounces orange juice

Toasted Coconut flakes, cashews, cocoa nibs, for garnish

AÇAÍ SMOOTHIE
THE BREAKFAST ROOM AT MAISON DE LA LUZ
LEON YOUNG SR., CHEF

Maison de la Luz is a distinctive new guest house from Atelier Ace. A place for reverie and proper Southern swoon, for prophetic visions or quiet inspiration, Maison de la Luz finds beauty in the curious and defines luxury as moving through the world with grace. The Breakfast Room at the Maison de la Luz is a private, guests-only dining room that is housed in the old City Hall Annex.

In a blender, blend all ingredients until smooth. Garnish with toasted coconut flakes, cashews, and cocoa nibs.

ABIGAIL RINAUDO, *RUSTON'S SWEETEST PEACH,* MIXED MEDIA
(THIRD PLACE SENIOR)

LIST OF PARTICIPATING RESTAURANTS

The Louisiana Restaurant Association Education Foundation and the George Rodrigue Foundation of the Arts are grateful to the following restaurants for their generosity in providing the recipes in this book.

ACME OYSTER HOUSE
724 Iberville Street
New Orleans, LA 70130
(504) 522-5973
www.acmeoyster.com

ALEX PATOUT
New Iberia, LA

ANDREA'S
3100 19th Street
Metairie, LA 70002
(504) 834-8583
www.andreasrestaurant.com

BENWOOD'S SURELY SOUTHERN
Mansfield, LA
www.benwoodssurelysouthern.com

BOURBON HOUSE
114 Bourbon Street
New Orleans, LA 70130
(504) 522-0111
www.bourbonhouse.com

BRENNAN'S
417 Royal Street
New Orleans, LA 70130
(504) 525-9711
www.brennansneworleans.com

CANE RIVER PECAN COMPANY
254 W Main Street
New Iberia, LA 70560
(800) 293-8710
www.caneriverpecan.com

CHARLEY G'S
3809 Ambassador Caffery Parkway
Lafayette, LA 70503
(337) 981-0108
www.charleygs.com

CHEF JOHN FOLSE CULINARY INSTITUTE
175 Bowie Road
Thibodaux, LA 70301
(985) 493-2700
www.nicholls.edu/culinary

CHICKEN AND CHAMPAGNE
New Orleans, LA
Instagram @chickenandchampagne

CITY PORK BRASSIERE & BAR
7327 Jefferson Highway
Baton Rouge, LA 70806
(225) 615-8880
www.citypork.com

COMMANDER'S PALACE
1403 Washington Avenue
New Orleans, LA 70130
(504) 899-8221
www.commanderspalace.com

COPPER VINE
1001 Poydras Street
New Orleans, LA 70112
(504) 208-9535
www.coppervine.com

DOMENICA
123 Baronne Street
New Orleans, LA 70112
(504) 648-6020
www.domenicarestaurant.com

FLANAGAN'S CREATIVE FOOD & DRINK
1111 Audubon Avenue
Thibodaux, LA 70431
(985) 447-7771
www.flanagansthibodaux.com

GABRIELLE RESTAURANT
2441 Orleans Avenue
New Orleans, LA 70119
(504) 603-2344
www.gabriellerestaurant.com

GALATOIRE'S
209 Bourbon Street
New Orleans, LA 70130
(504) 525-2021
www.galatoires.com

GW FINS
808 Bienville Street
New Orleans, LA 70112
(504) 581-3467
www.gwfins.com

HAZEL'S TEA PARLOR
700 S 3rd Street
Leesville, LA 71446
(337) 378-9080

**HOUMAS HOUSE PLANTATION
AND GARDENS**
40136 Louisiana 942
Darrow, LA 70725
(225) 473-9380
www.houmashouse.com

JACK DEMPSEY'S RESTAURANT
738 Poland Avenue
New Orleans, LA 70117
(504) 943-9914
www.jackdempseys.net

JACK ROSE
2031 Street Charles Avenue Floor 1
New Orleans, LA 70130
(504) 323-1500
www.jackroserestaurant.com

JOSEPHINE ESTELLE
600 Carondelet Street
New Orleans, LA 70130
(504) 930-3070
www.josephineestelle.com

JUBANS
3739 Perkins Road
Baton Rouge, LA 70808
(225) 346-8422
www.jubans.com

L'AUBERGE BATON ROUGE
777 L'Auberge Avenue
Baton Rouge, LA 70820
(225) 215-7777
www.lbatonrouge.com

LA PIZZERIA
3809 Ambassador Caffery Pkwy
Lafayette, LA 70503
(337) 989-4121
www.eatatlapizzeria.com

LA TRUFFE SAUVAGE
815 W. Bayou Pines Drive
Lake Charles, LA 70601
(337) 439-8364
www.thewildtruffle.com

LINK RESTAURANT GROUP
930 Tchoupitoulas Street
New Orleans, LA 70130
(504) 588-2189
www.linkrestaurantgroup.com

LOLA RESTAURANT
517 North New Hampshire Street
Covington, LA 70433
(985) 892-4992
www.lolacovington.com

MAGIC SEASONING BLENDS
720 Distributors Row
New Orleans, LA 70123
(504) 731-3590
www.magicseasoningblends.com

MANSURS ON THE BOULEVARD
5720 Corporate Blvd #A
Baton Rouge, LA 70808
(225) 923-3366
www.mansursontheboulevard.com

MARCELLO'S
340 Kaliste Saloom Road Suite C
Lafayette, LA 70508
(337) 235-1002
www.marcelloslafayette.com

MAYPOP
611 O'Keefe Avenue
New Orleans, LA 70113
(504) 518-6345
www.maypoprestaurant.com

MERIL
424 Girod Street
New Orleans, LA 70130
(504) 526-3745
www.emerilsrestaurants.com

MIDDENDORF'S
30160 Hwy 51 S
Manshac, LA 70421
(985) 386-6666
www.middendorfsrestaurant.com

MILK PUNCH MEDIA
New Orleans, LA
www.milkpunchmedia.com

**NEW ORLEANS CULINARY &
HOSPITALITY INSTITUTE (NOCHI)**
725 Howard Avenue
New Orleans, LA 70130
(504) 891-4060
www.nochi.org

P-BEAU'S QUALITY FOOD & DRINK
121 Bass Pro Boulevard
Denham Springs, LA 70726
(225) 271-8545
www.p-beaus.com

PALACE CAFE
605 Canal Street
New Orleans, LA 70130
(504) 523-1661
www.palacecafe.com

PARISH RESTAURANT
318 North 2nd Street
Monroe, LA 71201
(318) 376-2423
www.parishrestaurant.com

PHIL'S OYSTER BAR
4335 Perkins Road
Baton Rouge, LA 70808
(225) 924-3045
www.philsoysterbar.com

PJ'S COFFEE
New Orleans, LA
www.pjscoffee.com

PORTOBELLO'S GRILL
7622 Old Hammond Highway
Baton Rouge, LA 70809
(225) 923-3222
www.portobellos.net

RALPH'S ON THE PARK
900 City Park Avenue
New Orleans, LA 70119
(504) 488-1000
www.ralphsonthepark.com

RED FISH GRILL
115 Bourbon Street
New Orleans, LA 70130
(504) 598-1200
www.redfishgrill.com

RESTAURANT AUGUST
301 Tchoupitoulas Street
New Orleans, LA 70130
(504) 299-9777
www.restaurantaugust.com

RESTAURANT R'EVOLUTION
777 Bienville Street
New Orleans, LA 70130
(504) 553-2277
www.revolutionnola.com

ROCK N SAKÉ BAR & SUSHI
823 Fulton St.
New Orleans, LA 70130
(504) 581-7253
www.rocknsake.com

ROSEDALE
801 Rosedale Drive
New Orleans, LA 70124
(504) 309-9595
www.rosedalerestaurant.com

ROUJ CREOLE
7601 Bluebonnet Boulevard Suite 100
Baton Rouge, LA 70810
(225) 614-2400
www.roujcreole.com

SEAWORTHY
630 Carondelet Street
New Orleans, LA 70130
(504) 930-3071
www.seaworthynola.com

SHERATON NEW ORLEANS HOTEL
500 Canal Street
New Orleans, LA 70130
(504) 525-2500
www.marriott.com/en-us/hotels/msyis-sheraton-new-orleans-hotel/

SLAP YA MAMA
1679 West Main Street
Ville Platte, LA 70586
(800) 485-5217
www.slapyamama.com

SOLOU
7246 Perkins Road
Baton Rouge, LA 70808
(225) 256-7070
www.eatsolou.com

SPAHR'S SEAFOOD
3682 US-90
Des Allemands, LA 70030
(985) 758-1602
www.spahrsseafood.com

STAR CRAFT NOLA COCKTAILS AND ELIXIRS
New Orleans, LA
www.starcraftnola.square.site/

THE BREAKFAST ROOM AT LA MAISON DE LA LUZ
546 Carondelet Street
New Orleans, LA 70130
(504) 814-7720
www.maisondelaluz.com/guest-house/

THE SUSHI BAR CO.
528 N Columbia Street
Covington, LA 70433

TRILLY CHEESESTEAKS
3735 Ulloa Street
New Orleans, LA 70119
(504) 582-9057
www.trillycheesesteaks.com

TUJAGUE'S
429 Decatur Street
New Orleans, LA 70130
(504) 525-8676
www.tujaguesrestaurant.com

US UP NORTH
300 N Allen Ave
Shreveport, LA 71101
(318) 639-0022
www.usupnorth.com

VICTOR'S CAFETERIA
109 W Main Street
New Ibera, LA 70560
(337) 369-9924

VILLAGE CUISINE
8372 US-171 Suite B
Grand Cane, LA 71032
(318) 858-3200

VISIT BATON ROUGE
359 Third Street
Baton Rouge, LA 70801
(225) 383-1825
www.visitbatonrouge.com

WALK-ON'S SPORTS BISTREAUX
3838 Burbank Drive
Baton Rouge, LA 70808
(225) 757-8010
www.walk-ons.com

ZEA ROTISSERIE & BAR
5080 Pontchartrain Boulevard
New Orleans, LA 70118
(504) 885-5555
www.zearestaurants.com

ANNE ERWIN, *SWAMPY TREATS*, DIGITAL MEDIA

R